Basics of Ancient Ugaritic

MW00786108

Basics *of* Ancient Ugaritic

A CONCISE GRAMMAR, WORKBOOK, AND LEXICON

MICHAEL WILLIAMS

ZONDERVAN®

ZONDERVAN.com/
AUTHORTRACKER
follow your favorite authors

ZONDERVAN

Basics of Ancient Ugaritic
Copyright © 2012 by Michael Williams
Requests for information should be addressed to:

Zondervan, *Grand Rapids, Michigan 49530*

Library of Congress Cataloging-in-Publication Data

Williams, Michael James, 1956-
Basics of Ancient Ugaritic / Michael Williams.
p. cm.
Includes bibliographical references and index.
ISBN 978-0-310-49592-5 (pbk. : alk. paper)
1. Ugaritic Language–Grammar. 2. Ugaritic language–Texts. I. Title.
PJ4150.W55 2013
492'.6782421–dc23 2012028582
All Scripture quotations, unless otherwise indicated, are taken from The Holy Bible, *New International Version®, NIV®*. Copyright © 1973, 1978, 1984, 2011 by Biblica, Inc.™ Used by permission. All rights reserved worldwide.

Any Internet addresses (websites, blogs, etc.) and telephone numbers in this book are offered as a resource. They are not intended in any way to be or imply an endorsement by Zondervan, nor does Zondervan vouch for the content of these sites and numbers for the life of this book.

All rights reserved. No part of this publication may be reproduced, stored in a retrieval system, or transmitted in any form or by any means—electronic, mechanical, photocopy, recording, or any other—except for brief quotations in printed reviews, without the prior permission of the publisher.
Cover design: Tammy Johnson
Interior design: Michael Williams

Printed in the United States of America

12 13 14 15 16 17 18 19 20 21 22 23 24 25 /PHP/ 22 21 20 19 18 17 16 15 14 13 12 11 10 9 8 7 6 5 4 3 2 1

TABLE OF CONTENTS

Introduction 10

Nature of the Book 10
Uncertainty 10
Resources 10
Practice Exercises 11

Lesson 1: Ugarit in a Nutshell 12

The Place 12
A Brief History 12
The Literature 13
Intersections with Biblical Studies 14
For Further Study 25

Lesson 2: Language Basics 30

Orientation to Ugaritic 30
Writing Ugaritic 30
The Alphabet 31
Peculiarities 33
Exercises 34
For Further Study 34

Lesson 3: Nouns 38

Basic Form 38
Case 38
Gender 39
Definiteness 40
Number 40
State 41
Summary 43
Exercises 43
For Further Study 45

Lesson 4: Adjectives 47

Inflection 47
Types and Location 47
Comparatives and Superlatives 48

Participles 48
Exercises 50
For Further Study 51

Lesson 5: Prepositions.......... 52
Proclitic 52
Independent 54
Exercises 55
For Further Study 56

Lesson 6: Pronouns.......... 57
Independent Personal Pronouns 57
Pronoun Suffixes 58
Other Independent Pronouns 59
Exercises 60
For Further Study 61

Lesson 7: Verbs.......... 62
Tense 62
Qatala 62
Yaqtulu 63
Use 65
Exercises 65
For Further Study 67

Lesson 8: Moods.......... 69
Indicative 69
Energic 69
Jussive 70
Imperative 71
Exercises 72
For Further Study 75

Lesson 9: Infinitives.......... 76
Infinitive Construct 76
Infinitive Absolute 77
Exercises 78
For Further Study 79

Lesson 10: Thematic Stems 80

G Stem 80
Gt Stem 80
N Stem 81
D Stem 82
tD Stem 83
Š Stem 83
Št Stem 84
R Stem 84
L Stem 84
Summary of the Thematic Stems 85
Exercises 85
For Further Study 87

Lesson 11: Weak Verbs 88

Initial-*n* Verbs 88
LQḤ 89
Final-*n* Verbs 89
Initial-ʾ Verbs 89
Initial-*y/w* Verbs 90
HLK 91
Hollow Verbs 91
Final-*y* Verbs 92
Geminate Verbs 93
Doubly Weak Verbs 94
Exercises 94
For Further Study 95

Lesson 12: Adverbs 97

Adverbial Suffixes 97
Independent Adverbs 97
Exercises 99
For Further Study 99

Lesson 13: Miscellanea 100

Conjunctions 100
Words Expressing Existence or Non-Existence 101
Negators 101
Interrogatives 102
Vocatives 102
Attention Grabbers 103

Exercises 103
For Further Study 104

Appendices 105
Semitic Consonants 106
Text Designations 108
Vocabulary List 109
Additional Bibliography 128
Exercise Answer Key 135

ACKNOWLEDGMENTS

The need for this book became obvious after I wrestled for many years to make the currently available resources comprehensible to students who were making their initial forays into the wider world of Semitic languages extending beyond biblical Hebrew. The currently available grammars are simply too daunting for such novitiates. I acknowledge my indebtedness to the students at Calvin Theological Seminary, whose questions, comments, and suggestions over the years have contributed immensely to this presentation.

Steve Kline and Dan Vos, my two research assistants on this project, deserve special acknowledgment and thanks. Steve exerted painstaking efforts combing through the grammars and monographs to note agreements and disagreements, and the rationale for each. He also applied his well-honed editing skills to the writing itself to ensure this presentation of Ugaritic grammar was not compromised by English grammar or style. Dan also contributed to the usefulness of this book by doing many of the inglorious, but necessary, research tasks associated with its production.

I also must thank Verlyn Verbrugge and others at Zondervan, who courageously took on a project of this nature and were exceedingly helpful in seeing it through to successful completion.

This goal could not possibly have been reached without the steady encouragement, reassurance, and support of my dearest friend and wife, Dawn. Thankfully her genuine love entirely transcends the confines of any grammar.

My last acknowledgment pertains to the limitations of this work. These include limitations regarding its scope (concise, not exhaustive), its precision (due to unknowns or not-agreed-upon elements of grammar), and its audience (beginner, not seasoned scholar). I trust these limitations will not impede the book's usefulness in the hands of those for whom it is intended.

INTRODUCTION
Taking the "Ugh" Out of Ugaritic

Nature of the Book

This textbook is arranged in thirteen lessons to facilitate its use in a single semester. It differs from the standard grammars in its simplicity, clarity, and, occasionally, humor. The most important thing for students beginning their study of a new language is a textbook that introduces grammatical features as clearly and simply as possible, without sacrificing accuracy. I also wanted this textbook to be visually inviting, uncluttered, and easy to navigate. Moreover, I have decided that learning a new language does not have to be devoid of a few laughs. Just because the language is dead doesn't mean that those who study it have to behave as though *they* were.

Uncertainty

Despite what you might be led to believe by the confident statements in most grammars, there is still much that is uncertain about the Ugaritic language. Because the language was written without vowels, we are often making educated guesses about the vocalization of words. It is true that we have other Semitic languages to help us with those guesses, as well as some helpful features of the language itself that you'll learn about later, but these only go so far. Consequently, the paradigms you'll find in this introductory grammar are subject to correction and should not be read as though they were the final word on the matter.

Resources

I have drawn on the work of many grammarians who have presented comprehensive, though at times quite technical, analyses of the language. I have weighed their suggestions and have taken account of their agreements and disagreements. Most of the time, the grammatical aspects discussed in this book represent a consensus of scholarship. At times, however, when the data warrant, I present a minority view. Again, please remember that this is an introductory grammar for those just getting their feet wet in the ocean of Semitic language study. For those who wish to explore any grammatical feature more deeply, I have provided at the end of each lesson a list of resources that will facilitate your investigation. There is also an additional bibliography of other helpful resources near the end of the book.

Practice Exercises

It is regularly the case that Ugaritic grammars present concepts without providing beginning students an immediate opportunity to try their hand at using them. To facilitate learning and to enable you to enter into the world of Ugaritic texts as soon as possible, this grammar provides practice exercises at the end of each lesson. Wherever possible, the exercises are actual excerpts from the Baʿal and Anat cycle. So, completing the exercises will not only help you learn the grammatical concepts within each lesson but also give you the opportunity to begin translating real passages from a specific Ugaritic text.

LESSON 1: UGARIT IN A NUTSHELL

The Place

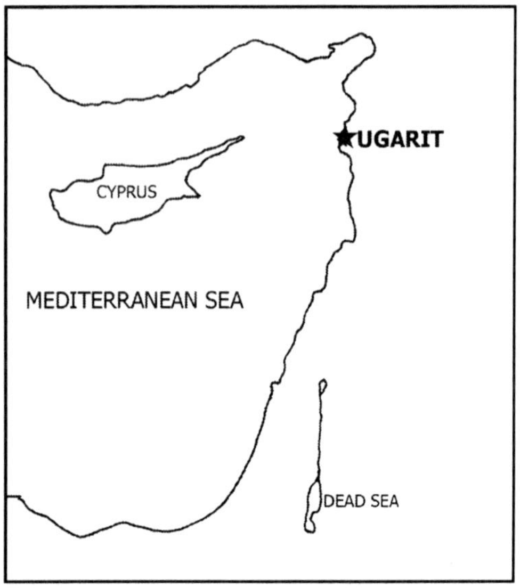

Ugarit was a cosmopolitan Canaanite city-state on the Mediterranean coast, almost directly east of the eastern tip of the island of Cyprus. It occupied a strategic and profitable position on the east-west trade route that connected the Mediterranean with the peoples of the mainland. It was also situated advantageously on the north-south trade route that connected Egypt with its neighbors to the north. This economically beneficial position also exposed Ugarit to foreign cultural influences and military pressures, and it was this last exposure that contributed to its downfall.

A Brief History

Although human settlement in the region of Ugarit dates back to the 8th millennium BC, for references to the proper name "Ugarit" we have to wait until at least the 18th century BC. Substantive documentation of its history appears even later, in the 14th century BC. Because Ugarit was in the middle of Levantine action, its history is inextricable from that of the surrounding nations. The precise dates for these events are still fuzzy (particularly for the reigns of the Ugaritic kings), but an outline of the history of Ugarit is provided below.

–1370	Ammištamru I reigns in Ugarit.
1370–1340	Niqmaddu II reigns in Ugarit.
	Ugarit nominally accepts the rule of Pharaoh Amenhotep IV (Akhenaten) but actually sides with the Hittites. The Tell el-Amarna letters witness to this double-dealing.
ca. 1350	The Hittite king Suppiluliumas conquers the kingdom of Mitanni and dominates northern Syria (including Ugarit).
1340–1330	Arhalbu reigns in Ugarit.
late 14th c.	An earthquake destroys the city and harbor. Ugarit never quite regains its former splendor.

1330–1260 Niqmepa reigns in Ugarit.
1274 Egypt (Ramses II) and the Hittites (Muwattallis II) fight to a draw at Kadesh and make a treaty. Ugarit remains under Hittite control and prospers during the subsequent time of peace.
1260–1230 Ammištamru II reigns in Ugarit.
1230–1210 Ibiranu reigns in Ugarit.
1210–1200 Niqmaddu III reigns in Ugarit.
1200–1190 Ammurapi reigns in Ugarit.
early 12th c. The "Sea Peoples" invade the region and subsequently burn and destroy Ugarit. One wave of their attacks reaches Egypt during the reigns of Merneptah and Ramses III. Ramses finally defeats the Sea Peoples in a great land-and-sea battle on the coast of Egypt, but he is unable to dislodge them from Canaan.

The Literature

In 1928, in the fields surrounding Ras Shamra (the contemporary name of Ugarit), a farmer's plow struck a stone. When the stone was lifted, an ancient tomb was discovered. This discovery prompted subsequent archaeological exploration in the surrounding region that, in turn, led to the discovery of clay tablets written in an unknown cuneiform script. Here begins the study of the language now called Ugaritic. Among the wide variety of tablets subsequently unearthed, the ones that have understandably attracted the most interest are the larger epic texts. These are few in number and consist of the legend of Aqhat, the legend of King Kirta, and the Baʿal and Anat cycle. The main outlines of these literary texts are provided below.

The Legend of Aqhat

The righteous, but childless king Danʾel is blessed with a son, Aqhat, in answer to his prayer to El and Baʿal.
Kothar-wa-Ḫasis gives Danʾel a bow of unusual quality, which he then gives to his son Aqhat.
Anat covets the bow, but Aqhat refuses to sell it to her despite her generous offers, the last of which is immortality.
Enraged, Anat transforms her henchman, Yaṭpan, into an eagle, and he kills Aqhat.
Danʾel has Baʿal bring down eagles and searches in them for Aqhat's remains.
Danʾel finds Aqhat's remains, buries them, and then mourns for his son for seven years.
With her father's blessing, Pūǵat, Aqhat's sister, goes out to avenge her brother.

The Legend of King Kirta (or, Keret)

Kirta mourns the loss of his palace, wife, and children.
Upon the advice of El, Kirta invades the town of Udum and, after negotiations with its king, marries the king's daughter.
El blesses Kirta and his new wife, at Baʿal's urging, and they have many sons and daughters.
Evidently as a consequence of his failure to fulfill an earlier vow to Asherah, Kirta falls ill (affecting the fertility of the fields).
El restores Kirta's health, with the help of the goddess Šaʿtiqat.
Kirta curses his son Yassib, who had taken steps to usurp his father's throne.

The Baʿal and Anat Cycle

Prince Sea, Yamm, goes to El to ask permission to build a palace.
He also requests that Baʿal be handed over to him, and El accedes.
Baʿal refuses and decides instead to meet Yamm in combat, armed with two magic clubs fashioned for him by Kothar-wa-Ḫasis.
Baʿal is victorious over Yamm.
Baʿal enlists the help of Anat, and then Asherah, to persuade El to let Baʿal have a palace.
El grants Baʿal's request, and Baʿal commissions Kothar-wa-Ḫasis to build a palace for him.
Baʿal's domination is usurped by Môt, and Baʿal dies.
Anat attacks Môt and conquers him.
Baʿal returns and resumes his rule.
Later Môt also returns and challenges Baʿal.
Môt finally acknowledges Baʿal's rule.

Intersections with Biblical Studies

One of the most exciting aspects of the study of Ugaritic for students of the Bible is the light it has the potential to shed on many aspects of biblical scholarship. Among these are the elucidation of the names and functions of deities, literary figures and concepts, textual difficulties, and perhaps even the thought world shared by the biblical writers. Summaries of a few of these details are provided below. Hopefully these will whet your appetite for the study of the language that has made such scintillating observations and suggestions possible.

Deities

Several of the Ugaritic deities are mentioned in the Bible. The Ugaritic texts provide us with more information about them than is possible to obtain intrabiblically. Some of the more significant of these include the following:

El

- Father of the gods and head of the Ugaritic pantheon
- Epithets include
  - *lṭpn il dpid* "the kindly one, El the merciful"
  - *ṯr il* "Bull El"
- Baʿal, Anat, Môt are among his children, born to him by Asherah.
- The gods are referred to in general as "the sons of El" or "the sons of Asherah."
- Creator of the world and its creatures (*ab adm* "father of humanity")
- Given the title "king"
- An aged deity who does not actively rule. He is active when it is necessary to decide on an important matter relative to the government of the world. Then the gods travel to his abode at "the mouth of the rivers" or "the midst of the channels of the two deeps."

  Cf. Ezek 28:2, where the king of Tyre regards himself as a deity and says: "I am [El], I sit on the throne of [the gods], in the heart of the seas."
- His abode is also described as situated on a cosmic mountain.

  Cf. Ps 48:1–2: "Great is the LORD, and most worthy of praise, in the city of our God, his holy mountain. Beautiful in its loftiness, the joy of the whole earth, like the heights of Zaphon is Mount Zion, the city of the Great King."
- Dominion of the world is divided between his three sons: Baʿal, Môt, and Yamm.
  - Baʿal rules the heavens (and the earth).
  - Môt rules the underworld.
  - Yamm rules the sea.
- Mentioned in connection with Melchizedek (Gen 14:18–20)?

  Cf. Gen 14:22: "I have sworn an oath to the LORD, God Most High [*ʾēl ʿelyôn*], Creator of heaven and earth."
- Cassuto, *The Goddess Anath*, 55: "It would seem that the children of Israel used to identify 'the most high god' of the Canaanites with their own One God. Since he was the highest of the deities and the maker of heaven and earth . . . the identification could be regarded as justifiable at least relatively."

In this regard, consider Gen 33:20, where Jacob set up an altar that he names: אֵל אֱלֹהֵי יִשְׂרָאֵל (*ʾēl ʾĕlōhê yiśrāʾēl*) "El, the God of Israel."

Baʿal

- His name means "lord"
- Major actor among the Ugaritic gods
- Defeats the sea god, Yamm, and the dragon, Lôtan
- His elevated position shows itself in his power over meteorological phenomena. Cf. the battle between Elijah and the prophets of Baʿal regarding the ability to produce rain (1 Kgs 17:1, 7, 14; 18:1, 2, 41–46).
    - So, he is often associated or identified with Hadad or Hadd (Ugaritic *hd*), the West Semitic weather god and leading deity of the Canaanite pantheon.
    - His association with fertility results in his being referred to as the son of Dagan (a West Semitic fertility god).
    - His rule guarantees the annual crops.
- Epithets include
    - *zbl bʿl arṣ* "prince, lord of the earth"
    - *aliyn bʿl* "powerful Baʿal"
    - *aliyn qrdm* "most powerful of the heroes"
    - *rkb ʿrpt* "rider of the clouds"

        Cf. Ps 68:4[5], for example, where this epithet is applied to יהוה: "Sing to God, sing in praise of his name, extol him who rides on the clouds; rejoice before him—his name is the LORD."
- His abode is on Mount Zaphon (cf. Ps 48:1–2[2–3], cited above)
    - The cosmic mountain *par excellence* in NW Semitic religions
    - This name transferred to Baʿal sanctuaries outside of Ugarit

        Cf., for example, the place name בַּעַל צְפֹן (*baʿal ṣĕpōn*) in the Exodus narrative (Exod 14:2, 9; Num 33:7)
- In the Bible, Baʿal is ubiquitous, appearing in references to
    - The temple of Baʿal (1 Kgs 16:32; 2 Kgs 10:21, 23, 25–27; 11:18)
    - The altar of Baʿal (Judg 6:25, 28, 30–32; 1 Kgs 16:32; 2 Kgs 21:3)
    - The pillar of Baʿal (2 Kgs 3:2; 10:27)
    - The prophets of Baʿal (1 Kgs 18:19, 22, 25, 40; 2 Kgs 10:19)
    - The priests of Baʿal (2 Kgs 11:18)

- Place names incorporating the name of Baʿal (for example, Baʿal Meon [Num 32:38], Baʿal Gad [Josh 11:17], and Baʿal Perazim [1 Chr 14:11])
- Personal names incorporating the name of Baʿal (for example, Baʿal-Hanan [Gen 36:38], Jerub-Baʿal [Judg 6:32], and Merib-Baʿal [1 Chr 8:34])

Anat

- Sister and consort of Baʿal
  - The mother of his offspring (although this has been alternatively explained)
    - A *bn ʿnt* may not refer to an actual child of Anat, but rather to someone who shares the attributes of Anat
- Volatile, independent, adolescent warrior and hunter
  - Distinguished for her heroic spirit and courage
  - Bloodthirsty and fierce in battle
- Epithets include
  - *btlt* "virgin," or "marriageable, adolescent female"
  - *aḫt bʿl* "sister of Baʿal"
- Appears in the Bible in
  - The personal name Shamgar ben Anat (Judg 3:31)
  - The personal name Anathoth (Neh 10:19[20])
  - The place name Beth Anat (Josh 19:38)
  - The place name Anathoth (Josh 21:18)
- A temple to Anat has been discovered at Beth Shan, and it is perhaps the place where the Philistines took Saul's armor after his death in battle (1 Sam 31:8–10).

Athirat/Asherah

- The great goddess
- The consort of El
- Her full name is *rbt aṯrt ym* "the Lady who marches upon the sea."
- Particularly worshiped in Tyre and Sidon, which helps us to understand Jezebel's actions (1 Kgs 16:31–32; 18:4, 13; 19:1–2)
- Epithets include
  - *qnyt ilm* "creator [f.] of the gods" (the deities are sometimes called her children)
  - *rbt* "Lady" (i.e., "great one" [f.])
- In the Bible, usually associated with a cultic pole
  - It can be set up/planted like a tree (Deut 16:21).
  - It can be chopped down (Deut 7:5).
- The Bible records other unspecified cult objects made for Asherah:
  - In 1 Kgs 15:13, we're told King Asa's grandmother, Maakah, made "a repulsive image [מִפְלֶצֶת *mipleṣet*] for the worship of Asherah."

  - In 2 Kgs 21:7, Manasseh sets up an image/idol (פֶּסֶל *pesel*) of Asherah in the temple of the LORD.
  - In 2 Kgs 23:4, Josiah orders the high priest to remove from the temple of the Lord "all the articles [כֵּלִים *kēlîm*] made for . . . Asherah."
  - In 2 Kgs 23:7, we find women "weaving" for Asherah.
- The Bible records 400 prophets of Asherah (1 Kgs 18:19).
- Her name is pluralized in the Bible to refer to goddesses in general (e.g., Exod 34:13; Isa 17:8; Jer 17:2; Mic 5:14[13]).

Yamm

- His name means "Sea"
- Represents the chaotic effect and power of water
- Closely associated with El
  - Referred to as "son" of El
  - Referred to as "beloved" of El
- Enemy of Baʿal over the issue of who should be granted a temple/palace
- Epithets include
  - *zbl ym* "Prince Sea"
  - *ṯpṭ nhr* "Judge River"
- Associated with (and perhaps occasionally identified with) various monsters (see below under "Literary Figures or Concepts"):
  - Lôtan (Heb. לִוְיָתָן *liwyātān*)
  - Tunnan (Heb. תַּנִּין *tannîn*)
  - Arishu and ʿAtiku
- The Bible contains many references to Sea (יָם *yām*) that allude to its mythological and cosmological significance.
  - Allusions to a cosmological battle with Sea (e.g., Ps 74:13–14; 89:9–10[10–11])
  - Allusions made in the description of the crossing of the Red Sea (e.g., Ps 77:16–20[17–21]; 106:9–10)
  - Allusions made in the description of the crossing of the Jordan River (e.g., Ps 114:1–5)
  - The chaotic power of Sea is also called to mind in contexts that assert the Lord's superiority over it.
    - Thus, in the symbolism of the architectural features of the Temple complex, the Sea must stand motionless, subdued, before the Lord (1 Kgs 7:23–26; and 2 Chr 4:2–10).
    - Thus, in the new heaven and the new earth, where all opposition to the Lord's rule has been removed, there will no longer be any threatening Sea (Rev 21:1).

Môt

- The god of death; his name means "death."
- The great swallower of life, the life of both gods and humans
  Cf. *KTU* 1.5 ii 2–4, where this great swallower is vividly described as having "a lip to the earth, a lip to the heavens . . . a tongue to the stars"
- Not worshiped like other deities in the Ugaritic pantheon
- Epithets include
  - *ydd il ǵzr* "beloved of El, the hero"
  - *bn ilm* "son of the gods"
- One of the main enemies of Baʿal (see the details of the Baʿal and Anat cycle above)
- In contrast to Baʿal's association with fertility, Môt is associated with death and decay.
- The Bible contains several possible allusions to Môt, in which he is personified as a kind of demon (demoted god) who reigns over Sheol.
  - His insatiability:
    - Prov 27:20: "Death and Destruction are never satisfied."
    - Hab 2:5: "Like death [מָוֶת *māwet*] is never satisfied."
  - His antipathy toward life:
    - Job 18:12–13: "Calamity is hungry for him; disaster is ready for him when he falls. It eats away parts of his skin; death's [מָוֶת *māwet*] firstborn devours his limbs."
    - Ps 49:14[15]: "They are like sheep and are destined to die; death [מָוֶת *māwet*] will be their shepherd."
  - The Bible presents this mythological enemy of life as ultimately overcome by the Lord of life:
    - Ps 49:15[16]: "God will redeem me from the realm of the dead."
    - Isa 25:8: "[the LORD] will swallow up death [מָוֶת *māwet*] forever."

Literary Figures or Concepts

Already in the previous discussion of Ugaritic deities, we have seen parallels to figures and concepts found in biblical texts; for example, the deity as the "Rider of the Clouds," Mount Ṣapān/Zaphon as the home of the deity, etc. In addition to these, several other literary figures encountered in Ugaritic texts may perhaps elucidate certain biblical passages. For illustrative purposes, just a few of these are briefly discussed below.

Danʾel / דנאל

This king of the legend of Aqhat is sometimes advanced as the referent in Ezek 14:14, 20; and 28:3. The biblical Daniel was Ezekiel's younger contemporary, yet Ezekiel refers to *dnʾl* as though he were a legendary character with universal recognition. Regarding the references in the book of Ezekiel, the *Dictionary of Deities and Demons in the Bible*, p. 220, suggests: "Since Daniel was not so well known as Noah and Job in Jewish circles, the post-exilic author was free to attach the name to a figure who would illustrate righteousness and wisdom in an historical context."

Lôtan / לִוְיָתָן

In the Ugaritic texts, Lôtan is depicted as a dragon-like monster who was defeated by Baʿal. Lôtan is described as a ***šlyṭ dšbʿt rašm*** "mighty one with seven heads"; a ***bṯn brḥ*** "fleeing serpent"; and a *bṯn ʿqltn* "crooked serpent"—designations that find parallels in biblical texts (see Isa 27:1 and Rev 12:3). Lôtan is often associated with Yamm and another mysterious aquatic monster, Tunnan. The distinctions between these entities are not always clear, and perhaps should not be sought.

In the Bible, Lôtan shows up as לִוְיָתָן (*liwyātān*)—commonly rendered "Leviathan." The monster Tunnan appears as תַּנִּין (*tannîn*) or, plural, תַּנִּינִים (*tannînîm*), or the hybrid תַּנִּים (*tannîm*). That the significations of Leviathan/Lôtan and Tunnan, as well as that of Yamm, romp in each other's semantic fields is evident from passages such as:

Job 7:12	הֲיָם־אָנִי אִם־תַּנִּין *hăyām-ʾānî ʾim-tannîn*	Am I [Yamm] or [Tunnan]?
Ps 74:13–14	אַתָּה פוֹרַרְתָּ בְעָזְּךָ יָם *ʾattâ pôrartā bĕʿozzĕkā yām*	It was you who split open [Yamm] by your power;
	שִׁבַּרְתָּ רָאשֵׁי תַנִּינִים עַל־הַמָּיִם *šibbartā rāʾšê tannînîm ʿal-hammāyim*	you broke the heads of [Tunnan] in the waters.
	אַתָּה רִצַּצְתָּ רָאשֵׁי לִוְיָתָן *ʾattâ riṣṣaṣtā rāʾšê liwyātān*	It was you who crushed the heads of [Lôtan].

These mythological beasts are linked in the Bible to the enemies of the Lord, which he defeats. For example, in Ezek 29:3, the king of Egypt is addressed as Tunnan: "I am against you, Pharaoh king of Egypt, you great [*tannîm*] lying among your streams." These beasts are also summoned in biblical texts to depict the great eschatological enemy of the Lord that will ultimately be slain. In Isa 27:1, for example, Lôtan/Leviathan and Tunnan rear their heads: "In that day, the LORD will punish with his sword . . . Leviathan the gliding serpent, Leviathan the coiling serpent; he will slay the [*tannîn*] of the sea." The New Testament carries forward this allusion to these Ugaritic mythological beasts in its depiction of the final battle between God and "an enormous red dragon with seven heads" (Rev 12:3). The Greek word translated as "dragon" is δράκων, a word the Septuagint consistently uses to translate *tannîn*.

Rapaʾūma / רְפָאִים

The Ugaritic texts indicate the *rapaʾūma* are inhabitants of the underworld and may be deified royal ancestors. In the legend of King Kirta, for example, Kirta mourns the loss of his whole family, who have become *rapaʾūma*. The ongoing function of the *rapaʾūma* is to watch over the dynastic continuity. Other Ugaritic texts suggest that *rapaʾu* (sg. of *rapaʾūma*) refers to manly vigor and vitality, an expected attribute of any king or leader. Thus, in the legend of Aqhat, Danʾel is regularly described as a *rapaʾu*, and this word is frequently a parallel to "hero."

In the Bible, the *rapaʾūma* of Ugaritic texts appear as *rĕpāʾîm*. As in the Ugaritic texts, they are inhabitants of the underworld, identified in some passages as deceased leaders and kings. Cf., for example, Isa 14:9:

שְׁאוֹל מִתַּחַת רָגְזָה לְךָ לִקְרַאת בּוֹאֶךָ *šĕʾôl mittaḥat rāgĕzâ lĕkā liqraʾt bôʾekā*	The realm of the dead below is all astir to meet you at your coming;
עוֹרֵר לְךָ רְפָאִים כָּל־עַתּוּדֵי אָרֶץ *ʿôrēr lĕkā rĕpāʾîm kol-ʿattûdê ʾāreṣ*	it rouses the [*rĕpāʾîm*] to greet you—all those who were leaders in the world;
הֵקִים מִכִּסְאוֹתָם כֹּל מַלְכֵי גוֹיִם *hēqîm mikkisʾôtām kōl malkê gôyim*	it makes them rise from their thrones—all those who were kings over the nations.

Occasionally in the Bible, the *rĕpāʾîm* are described as giants of the past. Cf., for example, the description of the bed of "the last of the Rephaites"—Og, king of Bashan (Deut 3:11): "His bed . . . was more than nine cubits long and four cubits wide." Admittedly, the size of his bed does not directly translate into *his* size, but it is logical to assume a similar scale. Perhaps this suggestion of abnormally large physical proportion is a projection of the significance of the *rĕpā'îm* as leaders or kings onto their physical dimensions.

Textual Insights

This intersection with biblical studies has the potential to explain many biblical difficulties by means of observed parallel lexemes, patterns, and constructions. This area of inquiry also has the potential to lead the unsuspecting down many dark alleys where the illegitimate practice (or neglect) of comparative Semitic grammar, liberal textual emendation, possibilities promoted as certainties, and all their unsavory friends are ready to rough up the unwary tourist. Nevertheless, when the pursuit of textual insights by means of a study of observed parallels between Ugaritic and biblical texts is conducted in a disciplined fashion, and is open to continual and rigorous examination and correction, its results can shed valuable light on biblical difficulties. Brief outlines for a few of these insights are provided below.

"Silver Dross" or "Glaze"?

כסף סיגים *ksp sygym* (Prov 26:23) is usually translated as "silver dross." "Dross" hardly suggests attractiveness. But the context seems to require that the word mean something that is attractive (to parallel "fervent lips") covering over or disguising something ugly (to parallel "an evil heart").

כֶּסֶף סִיגִים מְצֻפֶּה עַל־חָרֶשׂ *kesep sîgîm mĕṣuppeh ʿal-ḥāreś*	Like a coating of silver dross on earthenware
שְׂפָתַיִם דֹּלְקִים וְלֶב־רָע *śĕpātayim dōlĕqîm wĕleb-rāʿ*	are fervent lips with an evil heart

Thus, "silver dross" doesn't seem to make sense here. However, with a different word-division, the *k* can be understood to be the Ugaritic and Hebrew proclitic preposition meaning "like." *Spsygym* corresponds to a noun recognized in Ugaritic as *spsg*, meaning "glaze." Thus, with a different word-division in Hebrew to reflect the Ugaritic noun (i.e., כספס[י]ג[י]ם), the meaning could be "like glaze." "Glaze" would provide the "something that is attractive" that covers over "something ugly" ("earthenware"). This vocabulary item from Ugaritic may therefore provide an explanation for the biblical passage.

A "Wide House" or a "Noisy House"?

In Prov 21:9 and 25:24, we encounter the phrase בֵּית חָבֶר (*bêt ḥāber*).

טוֹב לָשֶׁבֶת עַל־פִּנַּת־גָּג *ṭôb lāšebet ʿal-pinnat-gāg*	Better to live on a corner of the roof
מֵאֵשֶׁת מִדְיָנִים וּבֵית חָבֶר *mēʾēšet midyānîm ûbêt ḥāber*	than share a [*ḥāḇer*] house with a quarrelsome wife.

Because no sense could be made of the three-letter root *ḥbr* in this context, it was assumed to be the result of the transposition (i.e., metathesis) of letters from the root *rḥb* "wide." A "wide house" in the second colon would provide a suitable contrast to "a corner of the roof" in the first. However, the discovery of the word *ḫbr* "noise" in Ugaritic (supported by its cognate in Akkadian) has opened up another possibility. Perhaps the biblical proverb is not contrasting a narrow versus a wide space, but a quiet versus a noisy space.

"Pierced" or "Grieved"?

Psalm 73:21 presents an interpretive difficulty because it contains a verb found only once in the Bible: אֶשְׁתּוֹנָן (*ʾeštônān*).

כִּי יִתְחַמֵּץ לְבָבִי *kî yitḥammēṣ lĕbābī*	When my heart was grieved
וְכִלְיוֹתַי אֶשְׁתּוֹנָן *wĕkilyôtay ʾeštônān*	and my spirit [*ʾeštônān*]

The three-letter root *šnn* in Hebrew is usually defined as "to sharpen." Thus, the *hitpaʿel* stem was thought to mean something like "pierced." Cf. the JPS Bible's footnote to this verse, which suggests "I was pierced through in my kidneys." However, in the Ugaritic legend of King Kirta, this three-letter root is found in a context of weeping (*CTA* 16 I:11–13):

ʿl abh yʿrb *ybky wyšnn* *ytn gh bky*	To his father he goes. He weeps *wyšnn*; he gives out his voice, weeping.

The verb *šnn* in the passage is bracketed by the verb *bky* "to weep," suggesting a similar meaning. Added to this is the common Semitic practice of seating the emotions in internal organs. We would therefore expect an emotion (such as "weeping") to be associated with the *kilyôt* "kidneys" of Ps 73:21. Thus, Ugaritic has provided another possible understanding of this biblical text.

Thought World

It is tempting when confronted with so many apparent parallels between the literature of Ugarit and the Bible to conclude, perhaps unconsciously, that the cultures that produced these works also shared a parallel "thought world" from which these literary parallels have sprung. However, we need to be very careful in our consideration of the "thought world" of ancient Ugarit (or any culture for that matter)! There are many limitations on our perceptions of any culture of the ancient Near East, and especially one that presents as many obstacles as the one associated with Ugarit. Such impediments to our understanding include, at least, the following.

1) Ugarit was a cosmopolitan city, not unlike modern New York. It was situated on trade routes utilized by many cultures with whom it came in contact and shared influences. Thus, specific phenomena purported to illustrate the "thought world" of Ugarit may well have originated in some other culture.

2) It is not clear to what degree specific aspects, behaviors, or abilities of the deities or other characters represented in the mythological or legendary literature actually reflect the understanding or beliefs of actual people in the culture in the practice of their everyday lives. Perhaps these texts were viewed as entertainingly archaic; as traditional (perhaps even canonical) texts no longer (if ever) having contemporary relevance; as quasi-official or religious texts justifying the actions of the few, though not embraced by the many; or any number of other possibilities.

3) Any talk of the "thought world" of a culture presupposes a cultural homogeneity that is unlikely to exist in the real world. Imagine if a person talked about the thought world of the American people. That world would likely look quite different in the minds of the urban city dwellers of Boston than in the minds of the rural farmers around Des Moines.

4) When a parallel phenomenon is observed between two cultures (say Ugarit and Israel), in order to determine who is borrowing from whom, we must first determine which culture holds claim to chronological priority for the specific phenomenon under consideration. This is not always easy to do. It is possible that both cultures borrowed from a third, or that the influence of one culture was mediated (and perhaps modified) by another before finding its way to a third. When borrowing is proposed, the direction and nature of the suggested borrowing should also be specified.

5) Before considering issues of borrowing from one culture to another, we must also establish that there was the possibility, at least, of contact between the two cultures. This contact in the case of Ugarit and Israel is complicated by chronological and geographical distance. However, artifacts, traditions, or descendants from an extinct culture could still communicate aspects of the culture to new arrivals with whom they come in contact. The circumstances in which this could actually occur should at least be posited.

6) Even if there is no possibility of actual contact, direct or indirect, between the two cultures (and even if there is), there is still the possibility that the two cultures might be exhibiting a parallel phenomenon due to the fact that human beings tend to think and act in roughly similar ways. In other words, could the parallel be nothing more than coincidence? Is there some degree of complexity that warrants our belief that it is something more?

In summary, there is indeed potential for the study of Ugaritic texts to yield significant insights into our understanding of biblical texts, both in terms of their meaning and in terms of the practices they narrate. However, care must be taken to avoid the many potential pitfalls. This care, unfortunately, has not always been taken, and often much of the crumbly results of poor scholarship must be removed before surer footing can be found.

Quite apart from any light it might shed on any other discipline, there is great value in the study of Ugaritic in its own right. Knowledge of the Ugaritic language is our passport to another world. This world is ancient and largely unfamiliar to most of us, and there is much to explore. As we begin our literary journey into this strange land, may we be informed, entertained, and amazed by the skill, the artistry, the complexity, and the drama to be found in the texts preserved for us by the careful scribes of the past, who have passed on to us a wonderful literary legacy.

For Further Study

Albright, William F. *Yahweh and the Gods of Canaan: A Historical Analysis of Two Contrasting Faiths*. Winona Lake, Ind.: Eisenbrauns, 1990.

A presentation of Canaanite religion in the Bronze Age (including a brief discussion of the pantheon of Ugarit) and the struggle between Yahweh and the gods of Canaan.

Avishur, Yitshak. *Comparative Studies in Biblical and Ugaritic Languages and Literatures*. Tel Aviv/Jaffa: Archaeological Center Publication, 2007.

A consideration of specific linguistic, stylistic, and literary parallels between Ugaritic and biblical Hebrew with a view toward how the former elucidate the latter. The studies are highly suggestive but at times speculative.

Barker, William D. "'And thus you brightened the heavens . . .': A New Translation of *KTU* 1.5 i 1–8 and Its Significance for Ugaritic and Biblical Studies." *Ugarit-Forschungen* 38 (2006): 41–52.

A fine discussion of the relationship of Ugaritic *ltn* and Hebrew לויתן.

Bienkowski, Piotr, and Alan Millard, eds. *Dictionary of the Ancient Near East*. Philadelphia: University of Pennsylvania Press, 2000.

A handy reference tool, although not nearly as comprehensive as the title implies. Articles include short bibliographies.

Binger, Tilde. *Asherah: Goddesses in Ugarit, Israel and the Old Testament*. Journal for the Study of the Old Testament: Supplement Series 232. Copenhagen International Seminar 2. Sheffield: Sheffield Academic Press, 1997.

Argues that the goddess Asherah in Ugarit, Israel, and the Old Testament is not one goddess but rather the top-ranking goddess in each culture. Includes detailed analysis of texts and the name/title "Asherah." Up front with methods (source criticism and historical criticism) and definitions.

Caquot, André, and Maurice Sznycer. *Ugaritic Religion*. Iconography of Religions 15: Mesopotamia and the Near East; fascicle 8. Leiden: Brill, 1980.

Mostly black-and-white plates with notes. Also a nice map of site on page 2.

Cassuto, Umberto. *The Goddess Anath: Canaanite Epics of the Patriarchal Age*. Translated by Israel Abrahams. Jerusalem: Magnes, 1971.

A discussion of the nature of the Ugaritic writings, the relationship between Ugaritic literature and the Bible, the epic of Baʿal, and an analysis and commentary on tablets and fragments of the latter.

Cho, Sang Youl. *Lesser Deities in the Ugaritic Texts and the Hebrew Bible: A Comparative Study of Their Nature and Roles*. Deities and Angels of the Ancient World 2. Piscataway, N. J.: Gorgias, 2007.

A comparative work on the nature and various roles of the lesser deities, the so-called angels, in the Ugaritic Texts and the Hebrew Bible, including their participation in the heavenly council and their relationship to the greater deities.

Craigie, Peter C. "Ugarit and the Bible: Progress and Regress in 50 Years of Literary Study." Pages 99–111 in *Ugarit in Retrospect*. Edited by Gordon D. Young. Winona Lake, Ind.: Eisenbrauns, 1981.

———. *Ugarit and the Old Testament*. Grand Rapids: Eerdmans, 1983.

Good introductory material. Includes an intriguing description of how the language was deciphered.

Curtis, Adrian. *Ugarit (Ras Shamra)*. Grand Rapids: Eerdmans, 1985.

Straightforward introduction to the history, culture, and literature of Ugarit.

Gray, John. *The Canaanites*. Ancient People and Places 38. London: Thames and Hudson, 1964.

Includes many drawings and plates with accompanying notes. Uses archaeological finds and texts (English translations only) to describe daily life, Canaanite society, and religion, with an emphasis on the fertility cycle. Good introduction.

Heltzer, M. "The Lands of the Gods (Temples) in Ugarit and Their Personnel." *Ugarit-Forschungen* 38 (2006): 341–46.

———. "Some Thoughts about the Last Days of Ugarit." *Ugarit-Forschungen* 37 (2005): 371–73.

Presents the available evidence that contributes to our understanding of the demise of a once great city-state.

Kapelrud, Arvid S. *The Ras Shamra Discoveries and the Old Testmament*. Translated by G. W. Anderson. Norman, Okla.: University of Oklahoma Press, 1963.

Argues that many features of Israelite religion cannot be understood without considering Canaanite religion through Ugaritic texts. Includes brief chapter outlining method and assumptions.

———. *The Violent Goddess: Anat in the Ras Shamra Texts*. Oslo: Universitetsforlaget, 1969.

Describes Anat as the leading lady of the cult always alongside Baʿal, and as goddess of battle. Identifies myths as the backbone of the cult and discusses Anat in relationship to fertility and mourning. Includes some Ugaritic passages with translations. Good, brief introduction to the stories of Anat.

Loretz, Oswald. "Ugaritisch-hebräische Symbiose der Gottesberge ***ṣapānu*** und Zion in Psalm 48 2c–3c." *Ugarit-Forschungen* 40 (2008): 489–505.

A discussion of the relationship of the divine mountain of Ugarit and that described in Psalm 48. An understanding of German is necessary.

———. "Der ugaritisch-hebräische Parallelismus ***rkb ʿrpt*** || ***rkb b ʿrbwt*** in Psalm 68,5." *Ugarit-Forschungen* 34 (2002): 521–26.

A discussion of the parallel expression "Rider of the Clouds" in Ugaritic literature and Psalm 68. An understanding of German is necessary.

Malul, Meir. *The Comparative Method in Ancient Near Eastern and Biblical Legal Studies*. AOAT 227. Neukirchen-Vluyn: Neukirchener Verlag, 1990.

An indispensable resource for understanding the guidelines for responsible comparative studies between cultures. This includes recognizing the possible nature and type of the relationship and the steps necessary to determine "coincidence versus uniqueness." He applies his principles to actual parallel phenomena.

Marsman, Hennie J. *Women in Ugarit and Israel: Their Social and Religious Position in the Context of the Ancient Near East*. Leiden: Brill, 2003.

Large volume (780 pages) comparing Ugarit and Israel. Concludes that, socially, women were equally underprivileged in Israel and Ugarit, but religiously, women in Israel were worse off than women in Ugarit.

Moor, Johannes C. de. *The Seasonal Pattern in the Ugaritic Myth of Baʿlu, According to the Version of Ilimilku*. Kevelaer: Butzon & Bercker, 1971.

Argues for the seasonal interpretation of this myth. Majority of book is presentation, translation, and detailed discussion of certain texts. Also includes a number of helpful tables and indexes.

Obermann, Julian. *How Daniel Was Blessed with a Son: An Incubation Scene in Ugaritic*. Baltimore: American Oriental Society, 1946.

Text, translation, and analysis of tablet D2 (30 pages). Helpful for study of this specific passage.

———. *Ugaritic Mythology: A Study of Its Leading Motifs*. New Haven, Conn.: Yale University Press, 1948.

Argues that the Baʿal and Anat cycle is a building saga and provides analysis of the text of 5AB from this perspective. Also discusses the alliance-enmity motif.

Pardee, Dennis. "The ʾAqhat Legend." Pages 343–56 in *The Context of Scripture*. Vol. 1: *Canonical Compositions from the Biblical World*. Edited by William W. Hallo and K. Lawson Younger Jr. Leiden: Brill, 2003.

For this Ugaritic text (and the following two), Pardee provides a brief introduction, an updated translation, significant explanatory notes, and cross-references to biblical parallels.

———"The Baʿlu Myth." Pages 241–74 in *The Context of Scripture*. Vol. 1: *Canonical Compositions from the Biblical World*. Edited by William W. Hallo and K. Lawson Younger Jr. Leiden: Brill, 2003.

———. "The Kirta Epic." Pages 333–43 in *The Context of Scripture*. Vol. 1: *Canonical Compositions from the Biblical World*. Edited by William W. Hallo and K. Lawson Younger Jr. Leiden: Brill, 2003.

Parker, Simon B. "The Literatures of Canaan, Ancient Israel, and Phoenicia: An Overview." Pages 2399–2410 in *Civilizations of the Ancient Near East*. Edited by Jack M. Sasson. Peabody, Mass.: Hendrickson, 1995.

Includes a wonderful and nontechnical description of the form and content of Ugaritic literature and its relationship to that of Israel and Phoenicia.

Smith, Mark S. *Untold Stories: The Bible and Ugaritic Studies in the Twentieth Century*. Peabody, Mass.: Hendrickson, 2001.

Stories (now told) about the lives and scholarship of certain Ugaritic scholars and about the contributions of Ugaritic studies to the study of the Bible in the twentieth century. Organized by time period with lots of helpful lists of resources and people.

———. "Myth and Mythmaking in Canaan and Ancient Israel." Pages 2031–41 in *Civilizations of the Ancient Near East*. Edited by Jack M. Sasson. Peabody, Mass.: Hendrickson, 1995.

The first half of this chapter is the most valuable for Ugaritic studies. In it, Smith discusses the Baʿal cycle, its cosmic-political vision, and the biblical mythic imagery related to it.

———. *The Ugaritic Baal Cycle*. Vol 1. Vetus Testamentum Supplements 55. Leiden: Brill, 1994.

Introduction and textual commentary on the first two tablets of the Ugaritic Baal cycle.

Smith, Mark S., and Wayne T. Pitard. *The Ugaritic Baal Cycle*. Vol 2. Vetus Testamentum Supplements 114. Leiden: Brill, 2009.

Introduction and textual commentary on the third and fourth tablets of the Ugaritic Baal cycle.

Soldt, Wildred H. van. "Ugarit: A Second Millennium Kingdom on the Mediterranean Coast." Pages 1255–66 in *Civilizations of the Ancient Near East*. Edited by Jack M. Sasson. Peabody, Mass.: Hendrickson, 1995.

A clear, accessible depiction of the physical characteristics of Ugarit and its environs, the number and attributes of Ugarit's citizens, Ugarit's relations with foreign powers, the city administration, the structure of Ugaritic society, its scribes, and its ultimate demise.

Toorn, Karel van der, Bob Becking, and Pieter W. van der Horst, eds. *Dictionary of Deities and Demons in the Bible*. 2nd rev. ed. Grand Rapids: Eerdmans, 1999.

Thorough descriptions of ancient Near Eastern suprahuman power brokers based on available textual evidence and available studies. Each article also includes a bibliography for further research.

Walls, Neal H. *The Goddess Anat in Ugaritic Myth*. Atlanta: Scholars Press, 1992.

Focuses on the symbolic role of Anat as a way to appreciate the symbolism of Ugaritic texts. Concludes that Anat is not simply the goddess of love and war; she is an adolescent female tomboy independent of male authority, representing a threat to society because she does not fulfill the prescribed roles of females.

Watson, W. G. E., and Nicolas Wyatt, eds., *Handbook for Ugaritic Studies*. Handbuch der Orientalistik 1/39. Leiden: Brill, 1999.

Chapters about language, literature, society, history, and religion. Good references and indexes.

Yon, Marguerite. *The City of Ugarit at Tell Ras Shamra*. Winona Lake, Ind.: Eisenbrauns, 2006.

Great pictures, drawings, and maps.

Yon, Marguerite, Pierre Bordreuil, and Dennis Pardee. "Ugarit." Pages 695–712 in vol. 6 of *The Anchor Bible Dictionary*. Edited by David Noel Freedman. 6 vols. New York: Doubleday, 1992.

Overview of history, archaeology, texts, and literature. Includes several helpful maps, charts, and images.

Young, Gordon, ed. *Ugarit in Retrospect: Fifty Years of Ugarit and Ugaritic*. Winona Lake, Ind.: Eisenbrauns, 1981.

Essays presented at the symposium commemorating fifty years of studying Ugarit and the Ugaritic language. Essays retrospectively reflect on the current state of Ugaritic studies.

Younger, K. Lawson Jr., ed. *Ugarit at Seventy-Five*. Winona Lake, Ind.: Eisenbrauns, 2007.

Essays presented at the conference commemorating seventy-five years of studying Ugarit and the Ugaritic language. Essays address specific texts as well as archaeological and historical issues.

LESSON 2: LANGUAGE BASICS

Orientation to Ugaritic

Ugaritic belongs to a family of languages called Semitic. This language family includes many languages, both modern and ancient, whose relationship to each other can be recognized by the common characteristics they share. All of these Semitic languages are presumed to have branched off from a common ancestor language, unimaginatively called Proto-Semitic. The Semitic language family includes Arabic, Ethiopic, Phoenician, Hebrew, Aramaic, Akkadian, and, of course, Ugaritic. Because Ugaritic is related to these other languages, we may use them to help us understand the particular sibling we are considering here. All of the Semitic languages share many grammatical features and even vocabulary. They may vocalize particular words a little differently and may, at times, use slightly different consonants, but knowing how these different languages all devolved from the common parent enables us to use them to determine the vocalization of Ugaritic words, which are written only with consonants. A chart that shows how the Ugaritic consonants appear in these other languages is provided for you near the end of this book (pp. 106–107). While you won't need to memorize or even use this chart to learn the basics of Ugaritic, it is a useful resource for further research.

Writing Ugaritic

While it is true that you will never have to write Ugaritic, you *will* need to know some details about how it was written by others so that you can correctly understand what they have left for us to read, as well as the difficulties associated with reading it.

Materials

Ugaritic was written by pressing the end of a cut reed into soft clay. The end of the reed was shaped like a wedge. Because the symbols of the language are thus wedge-shaped, the style of writing is called *cuneiform*—a word that simply means "wedge-shaped." By varying the shape, direction, and combination of the wedge-shaped impressions, the scribe was able to indicate different letters.

Direction

Ugaritic is usually written from left to right. Of course, there are exceptions, but these need not concern us. If you've already learned Hebrew, you'll have to remember to switch the direction of reading.

Consonants Only

Ugaritic is written using only consonants, not vowels. Wait; there's more! Doubled consonants are not indicated either. As you probably suspect, this can cause some interpretive difficulty for us. For example, if we did this in English, the letters "mt" could represent *met*, *mutt*, *mitt*, *mat*, *mite*, *mate*, *mute*, *mete*, *meet*, *meat*, or *mote*. We are dependent on the context to help us determine which word is intended. The context is usually sufficient to resolve any ambiguities.

Dividing Words

Ugaritic scribes usually (not always) indicated the division between words by using the symbol 𐎟. Even though (as we'll learn later) the conjunction "and" and some prepositions are attached directly to the word in Ugaritic, scribes occasionally separated these with the word divider too. In transliteration, this word divider is represented by a period.

The Alphabet

The following table indicates the cuneiform shape of each letter of the Ugaritic alphabet and the regular way that letter is represented (or "transliterated") in English.

CUNEIFORM SYMBOL	TRANSLITERATION
𐎀	*a* (or *ʾa*)
𐎛	*i* (or *ʾi*)
𐎜	*u* (or *ʾu*)
𐎁	*b*
𐎂	*g*
𐎄	*d*
𐎅	*ḏ*

𐎅	*h*
𐎆	*w*
𐎇	*z*
𐎈	*ḥ*
𐎃	*ḫ*
𐎉	*ṭ*
𐎑	*ẓ*
𐎊	*y*
𐎋	*k*
𐎍	*l*
𐎎	*m*
𐎐	*n*
𐎒	*s*
𐎝	*s̀*
𐎓	ʿ
𐎙	*ǵ*
𐎔	*p*
𐎕	*ṣ*
𐎖	*q*
𐎗	*r*
𐎌	*š*
𐎚	*t*
𐎘	*ṯ*

You may wonder what vowels are doing on the chart after we said Ugaritic only uses consonants. And if you weren't wondering before, you certainly are now. Well, the answer is that these aren't really vowels. Seriously. These are three different forms of the consonant ʾ. The vowel in transliteration represents the vowel accompanying the ʾ—*a* (representing ʾ*a*), *i/e* (representing ʾ*i*), or *u/o* (representing ʾ*u*). So, for words that contain the consonant ʾ, we get some help in determining which vowel is present. Normally, the form of the consonant ʾ indicates what vowel immediately *follows* it. Also, when the word calls for a vowelless ʾ, that is almost always represented by ʾ*i*.

Peculiarities

Ugaritic incorporates some regular peculiarities that one needs to learn in order to avoid difficulties in translating.

Diphthongs Contract

When a vowel and a consonant combine to produce a single sound, we call this a diphthong. For example, in English *o* and *w* frequently combine to the diphthong *ow*, producing a sound that is different than either of them has individually. But in Ugaritic, whenever certain vowels and consonants come together to form what would be a diphthong, the diphthong contracts.

1. *aw* always contracts to *ô*

Example: *mawtu* becomes *môtu*

2. *ay* always contracts to *ê*

Example: *baytu* becomes *bêtu*

Consonant Changes

When the consonant *n* comes before another nonguttural consonant (that is, any consonant except ʾ, *h*, *ḥ*, *ḫ*, or ʿ), it may assimilate into (i.e., turn into) that following consonant.

Example: ʾ*anta* becomes ʾ*atta*

Loss of ʾ*a* before ʿ

Because of the patterns present in the paradigms we will learn later, sometimes we would expect a word to begin with ʾ*a*. This is not a problem unless the word would have an ʿ immediately following the ʾ*a*. In those cases, the word at times eliminates the ʾ*a* entirely.

Example: *ʿaniyu* where we would expect *ʾaʿniyu*

In this example, the unexpected form *ʿaniyu* results from dropping the *ʾa* (resulting in *ʿniyu*), and then inserting an *a* between the *ʿ* and the *n* so that the word does not begin with two consonants (a big Semitic no-no).

Exercises

Transliterate the following Ugaritic words. Using the vocabulary list at the back of the book, supply the necessary vowels and then translate. Even though we'll be working with transliterations for the remainder of our study of Ugaritic grammar, it is good for you to gain a little familiarity with the actual cuneiform text.

1. 
2. 
3. 
4. 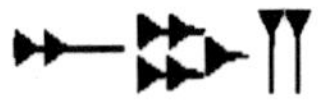
5. 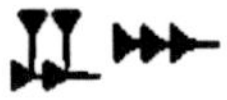
6. 
7. 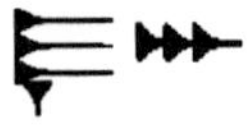
8. 
9. 
10. 

For Further Study

The Alphabet

Albright, W. F. "The Origin of the Alphabet and the Ugaritic ABC Again." *Bulletin of the American Schools of Oriental Research* 119 (1950): 23–25.

Cross, Frank Moore, and John Huehnergard. "The Alphabet on a Late Babylonian Cuneiform School Tablet." *Orientalia* 72/2 (2003): 223–28.

Response to Cross and Lambdin (1960), see below. Uses same principles to reconstruct the letter names from a tablet recently discovered with a presumably Aramaic alphabet. Includes discussion of each letter.

Cross, Frank Moore, and Thomas O. Lambdin. "A Ugaritic Abecedary and the Origins of the Proto-Canaanite Alphabet." *Bulletin of the American Schools of Oriental Research* 160 (1960): 21–26.

Explores the origin of the names of the signs/letters with reference to an abecedary tablet with Ugaritic and Akkadian signs.

Dietrich, Manfried, and Oswald Loretz. "The Cuneiform Alphabets of Ugarit." *Ugarit-Forschungen* 21 (1989): 101–12.

Helpful overview of the study of the origin and history of the alphabet. Reviews the state of the problem and recent publications, discusses arguments for the long and short alphabets, and, in the end, refutes the reduction theory.

———. "Die ugaritische Alphabet." *Ugarit-Forschungen* 18 (1986): 3–26.

Emerton, John A. "Some Notes on the Ugaritic Counterpart of the Arabic *GHAIN*." Pages 31–50 in *Studies in Philology in Honour of Ronald James Williams: A Festschrift*. Edited by Gerald E. Kadish and Geoffrey E. Freeman. Toronto: SSEA Publications, 1982.

Refutes the case against the existence of *ǵ* in Ugaritic. Examines twenty-three Ugaritic words that differ from Arabic in the use of *ǵ*. Helpful even without a knowledge of Arabic.

Grabbe, Lester L. "Hebrew *PĀʿAL*/Ugaritic *Bʿ L* and the Supposed *B*/*P* Interchange in Semitic." *Ugarit-Forschungen* 11 (1979): 307–14.

Discussion of different Semitic verbs for "to make/do." Argues that Ugaritic *bʿl* is unrelated to Hebrew *pʿl* (i.e., not an example of *b*/*p* interchange). Also discusses *nbš* and *npš* and warns against any "promiscuous interchange of *b* and *p*" based on these isolated examples. Concludes with some general linguistic principles and questions a philologist must ask when he or she observes *b* for *p*.

Greenstein, Edward L. "Another Attestation of Initial *h* > ʾ in West Semitic." *Journal of the Ancient Near Eastern Society of Columbia University* 5 (1973): 157–64.

Discusses a potential phonological relationship between the letters *h* and ʾ in Hebrew and Ugaritic.

Hallo, William W. "Isaiah 29:9–13 and the Ugaritic Abecedaries." *Journal of Biblical Literature* 77 (1958): 324–38.

Suggests two mnemonic devices (related to the ordering of the letters and the names of the letters) that may have contributed to the spread of the West Semitic writing system. Compares many alphabets with charts and discusses the discoveries of several abecedaries between 1945 and 1955. Briefly draws attention to Isaiah 29, which may refer to two West Semitic letter names: *ṣaw* and *qaw*.

Hodge, Carleton T. "The Hieratic Origin of the Ugaritic Alphabet." *Anthropological Linguistics* 11 (1969): 277–89.

Argues that the probable model for the Ugarit script was Egyptian hieratic. Includes an interesting chart comparing Ugaritic, hieratic, and hieroglyphic signs.

Jobling, W. J. "The Ugaritic Alphabet and the Khirbet es-Samra Ostracon." Pages 151–58 in *Ugarit and the Bible: Proceedings of the International*

Symposium on Ugarit and the Bible, Manchester, September 1992. Edited by George J. Brooke, Adrian H. W. Curtis, and John F. Healy. Ugaritisch-biblische Literatur 11. Münster: Ugarit-Verlag, 1994.

Discusses an inscribed piece of pottery from the late Roman pre-Islamic period written in a North Arabian script and the implications of this discovery for understanding the significance of the alphabet of Ugarit.

Segert, Stanislav. "Cuneiform Alphabets from Syria and Palestine" (review of Manfried Dietrich and Oswald Loretz, *Die Keilalphabete: Die phönizisch-kanaanäischen und altarabischen Alphabete in Ugarit*). *Journal of the American Oriental Society* 113 (1993): 82–91.

Helpful English summary of the book. Dietrich and Loretz conclude that a short alphabet coexisted with a longer alphabet. Segert concludes that the long alphabet was original and the short alphabet was a later development.

Speiser, Ephraim A. "A Note on Alphabetic Origins." *Bulletin of the American Schools of Oriental Research* 121 (1951): 17–21.

Some initial observations about the Ugaritic alphabet based on the discovery of an abecedary in 1949. Draws comparisons with other Semitic languages and posits how sounds may have changed over time.

Steiglitz, Robert R. "The Ugaritic Cuneiform and Canaanite Linear Alphabets." *Journal of Near Eastern Studies* 30 (1971): 135–39.

Concludes that these two alphabets come from the same proto-system, arguing on the basis on the graphic similarity of the signs. Includes tables that illustrate the similarities of the shapes.

Windfuhr, Gernot L. "The Cuneiform Signs of Ugarit." *Journal of Near Eastern Studies* 29 (1970): 48–51.

Brief introduction to the signs with a simple table that orders the signs according to their degree of complexity. Suggests that this was the original order and gives possible reasons for later rearrangement in the abecedarian order.

Consonants

Garr, W. Randall. "On Voicing and Devoicing in Ugaritic." *Journal of Near Eastern Studies* 45 (1986): 45–52.

Collects examples of the interchange of voiced/voiceless consonants (e.g., *b*/*p*) in order to discover whether rules govern these changes or they are simply variants. Concludes that there are regular rules of assimilation.

Reif, Joseph A. "The Loss of Consonantal Aleph in Ugaritic." *Journal of Semitic Studies* 4 (1959): 16–20.

Attempts to explain why Ugaritic has three *ʾālep*s and only one form of each of the other letters.

Vowels

Marcus, David. "The Three Alephs in Ugaritic." *Journal of the Ancient Near Eastern Society of Columbia University* 1 (1968): 50–60.

Explains Harold Ginsberg's understanding of the use of the *ʾālep*s in Ugaritic and lists examples to demonstrate that Ginsberg's theory is preferable to alternatives.

Sivan, Daniel. "Is There Vowel Harmony in Verbal Forms with Aleph in Ugaritic?" *Ugarit-Forschungen* 22 (1990): 313–15.

Suggests two possible instances of vowel harmony in forms of ***ydʿ*** and ***ʾrš***.

Tsumura, David Toshio. "Vowel Sandhi in Biblical Hebrew." *Zeitschrift für die alttestamentliche Wissenschaft* 109 (1997): 575–88.

Includes a two-page description of Ugaritic vowel sandhi (when one vowel swallows up the vowel next to it, because of either the vowel's dominance or position). Related to the loss of intervocalic *ʾālep* before *ʿayin*.

LESSON 3: NOUNS

Basic Form

Ugaritic usually forms its nouns from a root consisting of three consonants. Because it has this in common with other Semitic languages, those languages can be used to help determine what the vowels are for each noun.

Example: Hebrew נָהָר (*nāhār*) helps us to vocalize *nhr* in Ugaritic (where it has the same meaning).

Of course, there are exceptions. Some nouns seem to have only two consonants, and some (especially those borrowed from other languages) have four or more. At other times, certain consonants (which we don't need to get into now) are attached (or "affixed") to the three-letter root to make it a noun or to modify it in some way.

Case

Nouns have three cases (but, of course, only one at a time). We'll use the noun ***malku*** (king) to illustrate these.

Nominative: *malku*

The nominative case is used for nouns that are the subjects of sentences or are on the other side of a linking verb (a form of the verb "to be").

Example: *malku* sits on the throne.

Genitive/Dative: *malki*

The genitive/dative case is used for nouns that have prepositions or the word "of" in front of them.

Example: He sits on the throne of *malki*.

Accusative: *malka*

The accusative case is used for nouns that receive the action of the verb (these nouns are called direct objects).

Example: His subjects obey *malka*.

You no doubt noticed that all of the case endings for the singular noun are simple vowels: *u* for nominative, *i* for genitive/dative, and *a* for accusative. Sometimes, however, you will see an *-m* tacked on to the end of these singular nouns. This is called an *enclitic -m* and does not appear to add anything to the meaning. So why is it there? Perhaps to balance out a poetic line; perhaps to add emphasis; or perhaps to indicate something else that will eventually be discovered by you.

(Possible) Exceptions

For some obscure reason, some nouns apparently have only two case endings: the nominative and the accusative. The technical name for such a noun is a diptote (unsurprisingly meaning "two endings"). When diptotes find themselves in a position where the genitive/dative ending would normally be used, they use the accusative ending instead. The bad news is that there is no way to tell without context which nouns these are. So, just assume all nouns are normal unless you learn otherwise somewhere down the road.

Gender

Nouns are either masculine or feminine.

Masculine: no special endings beyond the case endings discussed above

Examples using the noun *malku* (meaning *king*):

malku (with a nominative case ending)
malki (with a genitive/dative case ending)
malka (with an accusative case ending)

Feminine: usually end with *-t* or *-at* (and then add the case ending)

Examples using the noun *malkatu* (meaning *queen*):

malkatu (with a nominative case ending)
malkati (with a genitive/dative case ending)
malkata (with an accusative case ending)

Exceptions

Some feminine nouns don't have the characteristic *-t* or *-at* ending, even though they are, in fact, feminine. Great. So how do you tell they're feminine? You can usually tell the true gender of these disguised nouns by the company they keep in the sentence. The verb or adjective associated with these nouns is required to be the same gender as the nouns and thus unmasks their true gender. We'll talk more about this later when we discuss agreement of subject and verb and agreement of adjectives and the nouns they modify.

Definiteness

Nouns are either definite or indefinite. "Definite" means that the noun is singled out from all other nouns and made specific in some way. There are three ways to do this.

The Definite Article

The easiest way to indicate definiteness is by using the definite article "the."

Example: *malku* the king

"The king" is a specific king and not any old king (or even any young king). You probably astutely observed that there is no *written* distinction between a noun that is translated with a definite article and a noun that is translated without one. We must depend on the context to determine whether the noun should be translated with the definite article or not. While that may be disappointing, it *is* just one less thing to learn.

Proper Nouns

Proper nouns are also definite, because names are given to specific things.

Example: He called the city *ʾUgarīta*.

Nouns with Pronoun Suffixes

Nouns with pronoun suffixes are also definite. Don't worry, you haven't missed anything; we'll learn about pronoun suffixes later. But it is obvious, isn't it, that if I am talking about *my* house, I am not talking about any house, but a very specific one.

Number

Any noun may be singular, plural, or dual. You might remember the dual from your study of Hebrew. If not, it should come as no surprise to learn that when a noun has a dual ending, the ending is simply indicating that there are *two* of those nouns.

Singular

We've already learned the forms for masculine and feminine singular nouns, so we can take a little rest here to gather our resolve for what lies ahead.

Plural

Masculine plural nouns end in *–ūma* in the nominative case and in *–īma* in every other case (note how the genitive/dative and accusative cases have the same form for the plural).

Examples:	The *malku* is coming.	The *malkūma* are coming.
	He wrote to one *malki*.	He wrote to many *malkīma*.
	He served one *malka*.	He served many *malkīma*.

Feminine plural nouns remove the *-t* (with following case ending) or *-at* (with following case ending) of the singular and replace it with *-ātu* in the nominative case and *-āti* in every other case (note again how the genitive/dative and accusative cases have the same form for the plural).

Examples:	The *malkatu* is coming.	The *malkātu* are coming.
	He wrote to one *malkati*.	He wrote to many *malkāti*.
	He served one *malkata*.	He served many *malkāti*.

Dual

Masculine dual nouns end in *-āmi* in the nominative case and in *-êmi* in every other case (note again how the genitive/dative and accusative cases have the same form for the dual).

Examples:	One *malku* is coming.	Two *malkāmi* are coming.
	He wrote to one *malki*.	He wrote to two *malkêmi*.
	He served one *malka*.	He served two *malkêmi*.

Feminine dual nouns keep the *-t* or the *-at* of their singular forms (with the case endings removed) and then add *-āmi* in the nominative case and *-êmi* in every other case (you guessed it, the genitive/dative and accusative cases once again have the same form for the dual).

Examples:	One *malkatu* is coming.	Two *malkatāmi* are coming.
	He wrote to one *malkati*.	He wrote to two *malkatêmi*.
	He served one *malkata*.	He served two *malkatêmi*.

State

Nouns are in one of two states.

Absolute

This is the normal form of nouns and so there is nothing new for us to learn. Let us take a moment to appreciate this.

Construct

When a noun is in the "construct" state, this means that it is connected to a *following* noun by the word "of." It is also important to note that every noun that comes after the "of" in a construct chain will have a genitive case ending. For example, in the phrase "the throne of the king," the word *throne* would be in the construct state and the word *king* would be in the normal, absolute state (with a genitive case ending).

The construct state is recognized by changes in the plural and dual forms of nouns. The singular nouns look the same in the absolute and construct state. So, for these nouns we have to determine that they're in construct (connected by "of" to a following word) by means of the context alone. For the plural and dual nouns, the change in the construct form involves *only* those forms that have an *m* in the ending. So, the feminine plural forms are unaffected. To get to the construct of forms with *m* in the ending, remove the part of the dual or plural ending from *m* to the end of the word.

All of that may have come at you a little fast. Try reading it again with the help of the following examples.

Examples: The single *malku* of the land.
The many *malkū* of the land.
He wrote to the many *malkī* of the land.
He served the many *malkī* of the land.
The two *malkā* of the land.
He wrote to the two *malkê* of the land.
He served the two *malkê* of the land.

The single *malkatu* of the land.
The many *malkātu* of the land.
He wrote to the many *malkāti* of the land.
He served the many *malkāti* of the land.
The two *malkatā* of the land.
He wrote to the two *malkatê* of the land.
He served the two *malkatê* of the land.

Remember, every noun that comes after the "of" in a construct chain will have a genitive case ending. Thus, in *all* of the examples above, the word "land" would have a genitive case ending (-*i*).

Exceptions

For obscure reasons, probably having to do with the enclitic *-m* discussed above (p. 39), the construct form of the word found in the text sometimes ends with an *-m*. Wait just a second. We just learned that the construct form drops off the *-m* of the dual and plural endings! That's right, but languages don't always behave. English is no exception. The plural of *house* is *houses*, but the plural of *mouse* is . . . well, *mice*. The fact is that it appears that sometimes in Ugaritic, the construct forms have an *-m*. This doesn't occur regularly or with any predictability. Of course not. That would make life too easy and therefore not as enjoyably challenging.

Summary

What we've learned about a noun's case, gender, number, and state is presented below in the following chart. It is absolutely essential that you understand these forms of the noun before going forward.

	SINGULAR		DUAL		PLURAL	
	ABSOLUTE	CONSTRUCT	ABSOLUTE	CONSTRUCT	ABSOLUTE	CONSTRUCT
MASCULINE NOMINATIVE	*malku*	*malku*	*malkāmi*	*malkā*	*malkūma*	*malkū*
MASCULINE GENITIVE/DATIVE	*malki*	*malki*	*malkêmi*	*malkê*	*malkīma*	*malkī*
MASCULINE ACCUSATIVE	*malka*	*malka*	*malkêmi*	*malkê*	*malkīma*	*malkī*
FEMININE NOMINATIVE	*malkatu*	*malkatu*	*malkatāmi*	*malkatā*	*malkātu*	*malkātu*
FEMININE GENITIVE/DATIVE	*malkati*	*malkati*	*malkatêmi*	*malkatê*	*malkāti*	*malkāti*
FEMININE ACCUSATIVE	*malkata*	*malkata*	*malkatêmi*	*malkatê*	*malkāti*	*malkāti*

Exercises

Using the following vocabulary words, fill in the blanks below with the appropriately vocalized form of the noun or nouns indicated underneath. Take care to provide the correct number, gender, and case in each instance. Where possible, these sentences are drawn directly from the Baʿal and Anat cycle.

ʾarṣu	land, earth
ʿênu	eye

ʾilu	god, El
baʿlu	lord, Baʿal
bêtu	house
binu	son
yadu	hand
yômu	day
ʿurpatu	cloud
pinnatu	vertebra

1. The ______________________________ had died.
lord of the earth

2. The ________________ of her back are weakened.
vertebrae

3. Let him build ____________ of cedars.
a house

4. The _________________________ responds.
son of the gods

5. ________________________ pass by.
Two days

6. There is no ___________ for ___________.
house Baʿal

7. The _______________________ are upon it.
eyes of Baʿal

8. Lift up the mountain on your ______________.
hands

9. The rider of the ______________ fears him.
clouds

10. The ________________________ are on the ________________________.
eyes of the gods house of Baʿal

For Further Study

Proper Names

Cooper, Alan, and Marvin H. Pope. "Divine Names and Epithets in the Ugarit Texts." Pages 333–469 in *Ras Shamra Parallels* 3. Analecta orientalia 51. Edited by Stan Rummel. Rome: Pontifical Biblical Institute, 1981.

Forty-two Ugaritic divine names and epithets, each with notes, bibliography, and suggested biblical parallels.

Huehnergard, John. *Ugaritic Vocabulary in Syllabic Transcription*. Harvard Semitic Studies 32. Atlanta: Scholars Press, 1987.

See pages 317–18 for the morphology of selected divine and month names.

Layton, Scott C. *Archaic Features of Canaanite Personal Names in the Hebrew Bible*. Harvard Semitic Monographs 47. Atlanta: Scholars Press, 1990.

Suggests and analyzes four archaic morphological features present in Canaanite personal names in the Hebrew Bible.

Pardee, Dennis. "Ugaritic Proper Nouns." *Archiv für Orientforschung* 36–37 (1989–90): 390–513.

Bibliographic information pertaining to a large number of proper nouns, including personal, month, divine, and geographical names. See volume 34 (1987) for an introduction to this bibliography.

Richardson, Mervyn Edwin John. "Ugaritic Place Names with Final *-y*." *Journal of Semitic Studies* 23 (1978): 298–315.

A comparison of the spelling of eighty-two Ugaritic place names that end in *-y* with the Akkadian spelling of those names. Special attention given to instances where the *y* may indicate a vowel, a feminine morpheme, or a directional marker.

Watson, Wilfred G. E. "Ugaritic Onomastics (1)." *Aula orientalis* 8 (1990): 113–27.

———. "Ugaritic Onomastics (2)." *Aula orientalis* 8 (1990): 243–50.

———. "Ugaritic Onomastics (3)." *Aula orientalis* 11 (1993): 213–22.

———. "Ugaritic Onomastics (4)." *Aula orientalis* 13 (1995): 217–29.

A series of articles about Ugaritic personal names.

Duals

Sivan, Daniel. "Dual Nouns in Ugaritic." *Journal of Semitic Studies* 28 (1983): 233–40.

Discussion of issues surrounding the identification and formation of dual forms. Concise discussion with good examples.

Nominal Endings / Case Endings

General Works

Moscati, Sabatino. "On Semitic Case-Endings." *Journal of Near Eastern Studies* 17 (1958): 142–44.

Argues that the singular case endings of Proto-Semitic are short rather than long vowels.

Sivan, Daniel. "Final Triphthongs and Final *Yu/a/i –Wu/a/i* Diphthongs in Ugaritic Nominal Forms." *Ugarit-Forschungen* 14 (1982): 209–18.

Argues that there is no way to predict whether these types of diphthongs and triphthongs would or would not contract.

Case Endings on Construct

Tuttle, Gary A. "Case Vowels on Masculine Singular Nouns in Construct in Ugaritic." Pages 253–68 in *Biblical and Near Eastern Studies: Essays in Honor of William Sanford LaSor*. Edited by Gary A. Tuttle. Grand Rapids: Eerdmans, 1978.

Argues that case vowels are retained on masculine singular nouns in construct. Clear and easy to follow.

Zevit, Ziony. "The Question of Case Endings on Ugaritic Nouns in Status Constructus." *Journal of Semitic Studies* 28 (1983): 225–32.

Suggests the early breakdown of case endings on Ugaritic construct nouns.

Enclitic *-m*

Emerton, John A. "Are There Examples of Enclitic *Mem* in the Hebrew Bible?" Pages 321–333 in *Texts, Temples, and Tradition: A Tribute to Menahem Haran*. Edited by Michael V. Fox et al. Winona Lake, Ind.: Eisenbrauns, 1996.

Argues that there are no clear examples of enclitic *-m* in the Hebrew Bible. No Ugaritic examples, but nevertheless an interesting introduction to the debate.

Hummel, Horace D. "Enclitic *Mem* in Early Northwest Semitic, Especially Hebrew." *Journal of Biblical Literature* 76 (1957): 85–107.

Primarily interested in the use of enclitic *-m* in the Hebrew Bible, but does summarize various understandings of the Ugaritic *-m*.

Pope, Marvin H. "Ugaritic Enclitic *-m*." *Journal of Cuneiform Studies* 5 (1951): 123–28.

Argues against the theory that the enclitic *-m* is adverbial and concludes that the function possible in all cases is stylistic or emphatic.

Watson, W. G. E. "Final *-m* in Ugaritic." *Aula orientalis* 10 (1992): 223–52.

———. "Final *-m* in Ugaritic Again." *Aula orientalis* 12 (1994): 95–103.

———. "Final *-m* in Ugaritic Yet Again." *Aula orientalis* 14 (1996): 259–68.

A series of three articles that list the occurrences of enclitic or final *m* and provide notes and references to the latest discussions of a particular text. In the first article, two possible functions of *-m* are suggested: a focusing particle and an adverbial ending.

LESSON 4: ADJECTIVES

Adjectives modify (i.e., tell us something about) nouns and pronouns.

Inflection

Don't panic. "Inflection" simply means the way a word looks with all of its extra endings, such as the case ending, the gender ending, and the number ending. Well, the good news is that we have nothing new to learn here because adjectives have exactly the same inflection as the nouns they modify. So, for example, if a noun is feminine, plural, and accusative, then the adjective modifying it is feminine, plural, and accusative. Pretty straightforward. The only exception to this nice agreement between adjective and noun is when the noun is in the dual form. Adjectives don't have a dual form, so if an adjective is modifying a dual noun, the adjective will be in the plural form. There, that wasn't so bad.

Types and Location

Where does one find the adjective in the sentence, and especially in relation to the noun it is modifying? Well, it depends on how the adjective is being used. There are three ways for an adjective to be used (just as in English, by the way).

Substantive

A substantive adjective is an adjective that basically functions as a noun. For example, in English if one talks about the land of the free and the home of the brave, the words "free" and "brave" are adjectives referring to "free people" and "brave people," but are simpler ways to express those ideas. Adjectives used in this way may be found in a sentence in all those places where true nouns may be found.

Example: *qāniyatu* *ʾilīma* — *The creator* (i.e., the creating one) of the gods

Attributive

An attributive adjective is an adjective that tells us something about a noun without forming a sentence to do so. For example, in English if one says, "the big boat," the adjective "big" tells us something about the boat without forming a sentence to do so. In Ugaritic, these adjectives are placed immediately after the nouns they modify.

Example: *ʿanātu maḥrūṯātu* *plowed* furrows

Predicative

A predicate adjective is an adjective that tells us something about a noun by forming a sentence to do so. For example, in English if one says, "The boat is big," the adjective "big" tells us something about the boat by forming a sentence to do so. These adjectives are separated from the nouns they modify by some form of the verb "to be" (expressed or implied); in Ugaritic they may be placed before or after the nouns they modify.

Example: *ḥayyu baʿlu* *Alive* is Baʿal (or, Baʿal is *alive*)

Comparatives and Superlatives

A comparative adjective is one that describes a comparison between two things. For example, in the sentence "The canoe is small," *small* is a predicative adjective. We can make this adjective comparative by adding *-er* to the end: "The canoe is smaller than the ship."

A superlative adjective is one that sets the noun it is modifying apart from all other nouns. For example, in the phrase "the small boat," *small* is an attributive adjective. We can make this adjective superlative by adding the ending *-est* to the end: "the smallest boat."

In Ugaritic, however, there is no change in form between a regular adjective and a comparative or superlative form of the adjective. It is only by the context that we can tell whether an adjective should be translated as a comparative or a superlative.

Example: *maḥmūdu ḫurāṣi* the *choicest* of gold

Participles

Participles are special kinds of adjectives called "verbal" adjectives, and their English form usually ends in *-ing*. Don't let the term "verbal" alarm you. Participles are inflected exactly like regular adjectives and, also like regular adjectives, are substantive, attributive, or predicative. So what makes them so special? Simply this: because they are *verbal* adjectives, they, like verbs, can take a direct object. For example, in English one may use the predicate adjective *good* in the following sentence: "He is good." Nothing surprising there. Now, let us use a participle, a verbal adjective, in place of the regular adjective: "He is writing." As you can see, the word *writing* is occupying the same place and performing the same function in the sentence as the word *good* in the first sentence. But because a participle is a *verbal* adjective, it can do one thing more than the first sentence—it can take a direct object: "He is writing *a book*."

Form (using the root *qtl*)

	ACTIVE PARTICIPLES	
	SINGULAR	PLURAL
MASCULINE	*qātil-* (*u/i/a*)	*qātil-* (*ūma/īma*)
FEMININE	*qātilat-* (*u/i/a*)	*qātilāt-* (*u/i*)

	PASSIVE PARTICIPLES	
	SINGULAR	PLURAL
MASCULINE	*qatūl-* (*u/i/a*) OR *maqtūl-* (*u/i/a*)	*qatūl-* (*ūma/īma*) OR *maqtūl-* (*ūma/īma*)
FEMININE	*qatūlat-* (*u/i/a*) OR *maqtūlat-* (*u/i/a*)	*qatūlāt-* (*u/i*) OR *maqtūlāt-* (*u/i*)

Voice

You no doubt noticed that the chart above includes both *active* and *passive* participles. These terms have absolutely nothing to do with time. Rather, these terms, technically called "voice," have to do with the direction of the action expressed by the participle. Active participles move the action forward, onto something else, while passive participles reflect the action back toward the subject. For example, in the sentence "He is *writing* the book," *writing* is an active participle that moves the action forward from the subject (*he*) to the direct object (*the book*). Contrarily, in the sentence "The book is *being written*," *being written* is a passive participle that reflects the action back toward the subject (*the book*).

Examples: *ʿabdu ʾāḫidu ʾulaṯa* — a servant *taking* a trowel

In this example, the action moves forward from the servant to the trowel. That is, the servant does the *taking.* Thus, this is an example of an active participle.

hadāmu parūšu babarri — a footstool *overlaid* with electrum

In this example, the action is reflected back toward the subject. That is, the footstool experiences the *overlaying.* Thus, this is an example of a passive participle.

Exercises

Locate the adjectives within the underlined portions of the following sentences and phrases. Note 1) whether they are regular or verbal adjectives, 2) their gender and number, and 3) whether they are being used substantively, predicatively, or attributively. For the definitions of unfamiliar words, consult the vocabulary list at the back of the book.

1. *ḫatūʾu huwa*

   He was vanquished

2. *ḥayyu...baʿlu*

   Baʿal is alive

3. O *bāniyu banūwāti*

   Creator of creatures

4. The *ʾilu dū piʾdi šāmiḫu*

   god of mercy is rejoicing

5. Let Baʿal rain upon *ʿanāti maḥrūṯāti*

   the plowed furrows

6. the abode of *kallāti kanūyāti*

   the named brides

7. the gifts of *qāniyati ʾilīma*

   the creator of the gods

8. like *ḥarbi laṭūšati*

   a sharpened sword

9. *ʾanūšātu pinnātu* of her back

   Weakened are the joints

10. *taḥummu ʾili ḥukmu*

    The word of El is wise

For Further Study

Participles

Kedar-Kopfstein, Benjamin. "Semantic Aspects of the Pattern ***qôṭēl***." *Hebrew Annual Review* 1 (1977): 155–76.

Demonstrates that words that exhibit the typical active participle vowel pattern can function verbally, nominally, or as some combination of the two.

LESSON 5: PREPOSITIONS

Prepositions come before (or, in the pre-position of) nouns, pronouns, or other substantives and indicate the relationship of one word to another. For example, "The Spirit of God was hovering *over* the waters"; "Let there be a vault *between* the waters"; and "So God . . . separated the water *under* the vault *from* the water *above* it." Some common prepositions are *at*, *by*, *for*, *from*, *in*, *into*, *on*, *to*, and *with*. It is very important to note that every preposition in Ugaritic gives the noun that follows it the genitive/dative case ending.

Proclitic

"Proclitic" is another one of those expensive grammatical words with a simple meaning. It just means that these prepositions are attached directly to the beginning of the word they are governing. There are three of these, with each one having a variety of possible meanings. The specific meaning in each instance is determined by the context.

bi-

Sometimes this preposition may be written with a *-mā* attached to the end (thus, *bimā*). This does not change its meaning in any recognizable way.

1. In/Into

Example: ***bi****ᶜurpāti* (in the clouds)

In this example, we see the genitive/dative case ending on the noun "clouds" (caused by the preposition *bi-*).

2. With

Examples: ***bi****ḥarbi tibqaᶜannannu* (with a sword she cleaves him)
nabbatu ***bi****kaspi* (adorned with silver)

In the first example, "with" indicates the instrument used.
In the second example, "with" indicates the material used.

3. From

Examples: *tabaᶜū* ***bi****bêtihū* (They departed from his house)
šitiyī . . . ***bi****kâsī ḫurāṣi* (Drink . . . from cups of gold)

In the first example, "from" indicates the starting place of action.
In the second example, "from" indicates the entire place of action.

4. On/Upon

Examples: ***bi**garni* (on the threshing floor)
***bi**šabiʿi yômīma* (on the seventh day)

In the first example, "on" indicates a location.
In the second example, "on" indicates a time.

5. Against

Example: *ʿalayat **bi**ʾabiya* (She went up against my father)

6. Among

Example: ***bi**yāridīma* (among those going down)

7. For (in the sense of payment for)

Example: *ʿašru šapūma **bi**ḫamši šamni* (ten *šapūma* for five [units of] oil)

8. After

Example: ***bi**šabʿi šanāti* (after seven years)

9. By (in the sense of measure)

Example: ***bi**ʾalpī šiddi* (by a distance of thousands of acres)

lê-

Sometimes this preposition may be written with a *-mā* attached to the end (thus, *lêmā*). This does not change its meaning in any recognizable way.

1. To

Examples: *šārihu **lê**ʾarṣi* (flashing to the earth)
***lê**rabbi kāhinīma* (to the chief of the priests)
*yalūdu binu **lê**ya* (a son is born to me)
*šabʿu **lê**šabʿīma* (seven onto seventy)

The first example uses "to" in the sense of motion toward.
The second example uses "to" in the sense of address.
The third example uses "to" to indicate an indirect object.
The fourth example uses "to" in the sense of "in addition to."

2. At

Examples: ***lêpaʿnê ʾili*** (at the feet of El)
lêqāli rapaʾīma (at the sound of the ghosts)

In the first example, "at" indicates a location.
In the second example, "at" indicates a time.

3. For

Examples: *ʾêna bêtu* ***lêbaʿli*** (There is no house for Baʿal)
waʾalpu ***lêʾakli*** (and an ox for food)

In the first example, "for" indicates possession.
In the second example, "for" indicates purpose.

4. By

Example: ***lêḥayyi*** *malki* (by the life of the king)

This sense for *lê-* is restricted to oath formulae like this.

5. From

Example: *yaridu* ***lêkussīʾi*** (He comes down from the throne)

6. On

Example: ***lêbâmati*** *ʿêri* (on the back of an ass)

ka- like, as

Sometimes this preposition may be written with a *-mā* attached to the end (thus, *kamā*). This does not change its meaning in any recognizable way.

Example: ***kaʾimmari*** *bipīhu* (like a lamb in his mouth)

Independent

"Independent" is a bit misleading. These prepositions still come directly before nouns and function together with them to form a modifying phrase. However, they are called "independent" because they are not *attached* to the noun, but are separate, independent words. These may be found in the vocabulary list at the end of this book. For now, however, several are provided below in the vocabulary list for this lesson so that you can practice your skills with both proclitic and independent prepositions.

Exercises

Using the following vocabulary words (and those from previous lessons), translate the Ugaritic words and phrases in the following sentences.

Nouns

našru	eagle
nāšu	man
nûratu	torch, luminary
panûma	face (plural in form)
paʿnu	foot

Prepositions

bi-	see above lesson
lê-	see above lesson
ka-	see above lesson
ʿimma	with, in the company of; to, toward
bêna	between, among
tôka	toward
taḥta	under, below, beneath; instead of

1. Do not draw near ***lêbini ʾilīma***

2. Strike ***bêna yadê*** Judge River

3. The club swoops ***biyadê baʿli kamā našri***

4. My life was absent ***bêna nāšīma***

5. She sets her face ***ʿimma nûrati ʾilīma***

6. There is no ***bêtu lêbaʿli kamā ʾilīma***

7. You must set your ***panîma tôka*** his city

8. They fall ***taḥta paʿnê baʿli***

For Further Study

Pardee, Dennis. “The Preposition in Ugaritic.” *Ugarit-Forschungen* 7 (1975): 329–78.

Description and analysis of verb/preposition combinations. Includes a history of the discussion of the Ugaritic preposition system and a large list of combinations with text and translation. Continues in *UF* 8.

———. “The Preposition in Ugaritic.” *Ugarit-Forschungen* 8 (1976): 215–322.

A continuation of Pardee’s article in *UF* 7. Discusses combinations of verbs and prepositions. Disputes Mitchell Dahood’s assumption that prepositions are ambiguous and interchangeable. Analyzes verbs in nominal clauses, extended forms of prepositions, and complex prepositions. Includes interesting graphs that illustrate the semantic field of several prepositions.

———. “More on the Preposition in Ugaritic.” *Ugarit-Forschungen* 11 (1979): 685–92.

List of verb/preposition combinations in texts published from 1972 to 1979. The author notes no new nuances in these usages.

Pope, Marvin H. “A Resurvey of Some Ugaritic-Hebrew Connections.” Pages 351–57 in *Probative Pontificating in Ugaritic and Biblical Literature: Collected Essays.* Ugaritisch-biblische Literatur 10. Edited by M. S. Smith. Münster: Ugarit-Verlag, 1994.

Includes comments about and examples of the prepositions *l* and *tḥt*.

Rainey, Anson F. “Some Prepositional Nuances in Ugaritic Administrative Texts.” Pages 205–11 in *Proceedings of the International Conference on Semitic Studies Held in Jerusalem, 19–23 July 1965*. Jerusalem: The Israel Academy of Sciences and Humanities, 1969.

Survey of how certain prepositions were used in contracts and other administrative texts.

LESSON 6: PRONOUNS

Independent Personal Pronouns

Pronouns stand in the place of nouns and have the same gender and number as the nouns to which they refer. Personal pronouns are pronouns that usually refer to persons. Independent personal pronouns are personal pronouns that are not suffixes, but rather stand alone as separate words. In English, the independent personal pronouns are *I*, *you* (for both individuals and groups), *he*, *she*, *it*, *we*, and *they*. Ugaritic personal pronouns are displayed in the table below, along with an example for each one.

SINGULAR INDEPENDENT PERSONAL PRONOUNS

1ST PERSON MASCULINE or FEMININE	*ʾanā* *ʾanāku*	*ʾanā ʾittaliku* *ʾaṯibanna ʾanāku*	**I** have walked **I** will sit down
2ND PERSON MASCULINE	*ʾatta*	*ʾatta ʾayyumarru*	**You** are Ayyumarru
2ND PERSON FEMININE	*ʾatti*	*ṣiʾ ʾatti . . . ʾamatu yariḫ*	Go out, **you** . . . (fem.) slave of Yariḫ!
3RD PERSON MASCULINE	*huwa*[1]	*huwa yabilu ʾargamanaka*	**He** must bring your tribute
3RD PERSON FEMININE	*hiya*[2]	*maǵāyu hiya*	**She** arrived

PLURAL INDEPENDENT PERSONAL PRONOUNS

1ST PERSON MASCULINE or FEMININE		Unattested
2ND PERSON MASCULINE	[*ʾattum*]	Not attested with certainty
2ND PERSON FEMININE		Unattested
3RD PERSON MASCULINE	[*hum*[3]]	Not attested with certainty
3RD PERSON FEMININE	[*hinna*]	Not attested with certainty

DUAL INDEPENDENT PERSONAL PRONOUNS

2ND PERSON MASCULINE or FEMININE	*ʾattumā*	*ʾattumā baššatumā*	**You** (two) delayed
3RD PERSON MASCULINE or FEMININE	*humā*[4]	*wanagašā humā*	**They** (two) drew near

[1]This pronoun also occurs in a non-nominative form (*huwati*).

[2]This pronoun also occurs in a non-nominative form (*hiyati*).

[3]It is suggested that this pronoun also occurs in a non-nominative form (*humūti*).

[4]This pronoun also occurs in a non-nominative form (*humāti*).

Pronoun Suffixes

Unlike English, but like Hebrew and Aramaic, Ugaritic pronouns may also be attached as suffixes directly to the end of nouns and verbal forms. Pronoun suffixes are usually called "pronominal" suffixes, but this is just a more intimidating way of saying pronoun suffixes. The forms of these pronoun suffixes are provided in the table below, along with an example for each one.

SINGULAR PRONOUN SUFFIXES

1ST PERSON MASCULINE or FEMININE	–*ī* –*ya*[5] –*nī*	*napšī ḫasarat* *lêbiniya* *yiqraʾunī*	**my** life was absent to **my** son he calls **me**
2ND PERSON MASCULINE	–*ka*	*ʿabduka*	**your** servant
2ND PERSON FEMININE	–*ki*	*taḥummu ʾabiki*	the message of **your** father
3RD PERSON MASCULINE	–*hu*[6]	*muẓlalu binihu*	the shelter of **his** son
3RD PERSON FEMININE	–*ha*	*bipîha*	from **her** mouth

PLURAL PRONOUN SUFFIXES

1ST PERSON MASCULINE or FEMININE	–*nū*	*malkunū baʿlu*	**our** king is Baʿal
2ND PERSON MASCULINE	–*kum*	*taḥummu yammi baʿlikum*	message of Sea, **your** lord
2ND PERSON FEMININE	[–*kinna*]	Not attested with certainty	
3RD PERSON MASCULINE	–*hum*	*taǵliyū ʾilūma raʾšātihum*	the gods lower **their** heads
3RD PERSON FEMININE	–*hinna*	*ṣaǵūratahinna ʾabkuruna*	**their** youngest (fem.) I name as firstborn

DUAL PRONOUN SUFFIXES

1ST PERSON MASCULINE or FEMININE	–*nayā*	*ʿimmanayā*	with **us** (two)
2ND PERSON MASCULINE or FEMININE	–*kumā*	*yaʿdubukumā kaʾimmari*	he will make **you** (two) like a lamb
3RD PERSON MASCULINE or FEMININE	–*humā*	*wayipʿaru šumatêhumā*	he proclaims **their** (two) names

---

[5]A noun in the nominative case uses the 1cs suffix -*ī* (which takes the place of the nominative -*u*). A noun in the genitive or accusative case takes the 1cs suffix -*ya*. The accusative form of the 1st person pronoun suffix on verbs is usually -*nī*.

[6]Other 3rd person masculine singular pronoun suffixes of uncertain vocalization are those that begin with (or consist entirely of) an *n*, and include –*n*, –*nh*, and –*nn*. This *n* may be associated with the energic form of the verb (described below).

Other Independent Pronouns

Not all pronouns are personal. Some are downright impersonal; they can be used to represent any old thing. Just as in English, Ugaritic has quite an assortment of these.

Relative Pronoun

A relative pronoun is one that introduces a clause that specifies something about the noun just mentioned. For example, in the sentence "The book, which I just read, is back in the library" we learn something about the book by the clause introduced by "which." In Ugaritic, the relative pronoun may have one of three forms, depending on whether it is referring back to a masculine, feminine, or plural noun.

Masculine Singular: *dū* (nominative)
dī (genitive/dative)
dā (accusative)

Examples:	*ʾêna dū ʿalênahu*	There is not **one who** is above him
	dī yakâninuhu	to **the one who** created him
	tinū dā taqûhu	Give **the one whom** you harbor

Feminine Singular: *dātu* (nominative)
dāti (genitive/dative)
dāta (accusative)

Examples:	*kêtu dātu ribbatêmi*	An altar (**which is**) of 20,000 (shekels)
	bahataya banêtu dāta kaspi	I have built my house (**which is**) of silver

Common Plural: *dūtu* (nominative)
dūti (genitive/accusative)

Examples:	*rāʿiyūma dūtu bâdê ʾiyatalmi*	The shepherds **who** are in the hands of (= under the supervision of) ʾIyatalmu
	binašīma dūti ʾiṯê ʾalpūma lahum	With men with **whom** there are (= who have) oxen

Demonstrative Pronoun: *hānādū*

A demonstrative pronoun is one that requires some demonstration when it is said. For example, if I say "this tree," then everyone looks at me to see where I'm pointing (or demonstrating). A *near* demonstrative indicates something near (*this* or *these*); a *far* demonstrative indicates something far away (*that* or *those*). There is no clear example of the far demonstrative in Ugaritic.

Example: *sipru hānādū* **this** document

General Relative Pronoun: *mannuma* (occasionally only *mannu*)

This is an all-purpose pronoun meaning *whoever/whichever* (when referring to people) or *whatever* (when referring to things).

Examples: *mannuma šāʾilūma* **whichever** inquirers
mannuma rigmu **whatever** matter

This pronoun may even be combined with pronoun suffixes to add indefiniteness.

Examples: *mannuka* **whoever** you(ms) are
mannukumū **whoever** you(mp) are

Interrogative Relative Pronoun

This pronoun has two forms, a personal and an impersonal, depending on whether one is referring to a person (personal) or a thing (impersonal). These two forms may also be found with an additional *-ma* attached to the end.

Examples: *mannu ʾêbu* **which** enemy? (personal form)
mīnu yarḫu **which** month? (impersonal form)

Interrogative Pronouns

There are two of these, again depending on whether one is referring to a person ("who") or a thing ("what").

Examples: *mīya biʾilīma* **Who** among the gods...?
maha yiqqaḥu **What** does he get?

Exercises

Vocalize and translate the Ugaritic words and phrases in the following passages. Underline the independent and suffixed pronouns. For the definitions of unfamiliar words, consult the vocabulary list at the back of the book.

1. *ank* made him *kimr bpy*

2. *tḥmk il ḥkm*

3. *mh* do you want *btlt ʿnt*?

4. Give *ilm d* you harbor

5. *mnm dbbm d msdt arṣ*

6. *aliyn bʿl ṯpṭn*

7. *klb arḫ lʿglh*

8. *ʿn bʿl qdm ydh*

For Further Study

Hasselbach, Rebecca. "Demonstratives in Semitic." *Journal of the Americal Oriental Society* 127 (2007): 1–27.

Ugaritic demonstratives are included in her discussion.

Loewenstamm, Samuel E. *Comparative Studies in Biblical and Ancient Oriental Literatures*. Alter Orient und Altes Testament 204. Kevelaer: Butzon & Bercker; Neukirchen-Vluyn: Neukirchener Verlag, 1980.

See pages 55–77 for notes on each pronoun, including suggestions for vocalization and use based on other Semitic languages. Even without knowing these other languages, the chapter is still easy to follow.

Zewi, Tamar. "The Definition of the Copula and the Role of the 3rd Independent Personal Pronouns in Nominal Sentences of Semitic Languages." *Folia Linguistica Historica* 17 (1996): 41–55.

Argues that the independent third-person pronouns, especially in early or classical stages of Semitic languages, did not function as copulae. No Ugaritic examples, but several from biblical Hebrew.

LESSON 7: VERBS

Tense

It is not at all clear that we should regard Ugaritic verbs with the same notions of tense that confront us in Western grammars. Some suggest that, like Hebrew, we should view Ugaritic from the standpoint of "aspects" or perspective on the action rather than "tenses." In this view, the action expressed by the verb is either regarded as complete (in the past, present, or future) or as not complete (in the past, present, or future). An action that a speaker or writer regards as complete is expressed by the *qatala* conjugation (a name arrived at by using the root *qtl* and supplying the vowels of the 3ms). This "aspect" is also, at times, referred to as the "perfect," but, again, this has the problem of applying a Western grammatical category to a non-Western, Semitic verbal system to which it may not correspond. Because this aspect is viewed as referring to a complete action, it often corresponds to our English past tense (or perfect, or pluperfect), and is usually translated this way—though flexibility in translation is required inasmuch as this aspect is not considered to be directly linked with time. An action that a speaker or writer regards as incomplete is expressed by the *yaqtulu* conjugation (a name arrived at by using the root *qtl* and supplying the vowels of the 3ms). This aspect is also called the "imperfect," but, of course, this may not be the best term for the reasons already discussed. Because this aspect is viewed as referring to incomplete action, it often corresponds to our English present or future tense, and is usually translated this way—though, once again, it is not at all clear that this aspect is directly linked with time.

Nevertheless, there seems to be a growing consensus that Ugaritic does, in fact, operate according to tenses and not aspects. This is particularly true of prose texts. Even so, there is certainly greater flexibility in the use of the tenses than that with which we are accustomed. For example, the *qatala* can be used to express the past, present, or future. The *yaqtulu* can be used to express the past, present, or future. As one might suspect, the exact details of the tense system are still being ironed out. For ease of reference we'll use the term "tense" here to refer to the two major types of Ugaritic verbs.

Qatala

Form

We will use the three-letter root *qtl* to demonstrate the conjugation of this tense, but, of course, the same conjugation will apply to any three-letter root. The jury is still out regarding the definitive vocalization of some of the forms in this conjugation. We are dependent to a great degree on parallel patterns in cognate languages. For our purposes, however, we provide a paradigm for practical use, with the realization that it may require some modification as the knowledge of Ugaritic increases.

SINGULAR		PLURAL
qatala	3rd MASCULINE	*qatalū*
qatalat	3rd FEMININE	*qatalā*
qatalta	2nd MASCULINE	*qataltum*
qatalti	2nd FEMININE	*qataltinna*
qataltu	1st COMMON	*qatalnū*

DUAL	
3rd MASCULINE	*qatalā*
3rd FEMININE	*qataltā*
2nd COMMON	*qataltumā*
1st COMMON	*qatalnayā*

Patterns

Normally, the second vowel (the theme vowel) of the verb form is an *a*. However, if the second or third root letter is a guttural, then the theme vowel is an *i*.

Examples:	*napšī ḫasarat*	My life (fs) was absent.
	ʿanatu wabaʿlu tabiʿā	Anat and Baʿal departed.

It is also important to remember that *ay* always contracts to *ê* at the end of a syllable. Why, you ask? Because in this conjugation, verbs whose roots end in *-y* may end up with an *-ay* before the ending of the *qatala*.

Examples:	*maǵêtu lêʾarṣi debīri*	I came to the land of Debir.
	ṯanêtu lêrākibi ʿurpāti	I repeat to the Rider of the Clouds.

(Notice how what would have been *maǵaytu* or *ṯanaytu* has contracted. We can tell this has happened because the *y* is no longer written in the consonantal text.)

Yaqtulu

Form

We will use the three-letter root *qtl* to demonstrate the conjugation of this tense, but, of course, the same conjugation will apply to any three-letter root. The jury is still out regarding the definitive vocalization of some of the forms in this conjugation. We are dependent to a great degree on parallel patterns in cognate languages. For our purposes, however, we provide a paradigm for practical use, with the realization that it may require some modification as the knowledge of Ugaritic increases.

SINGULAR		PLURAL
yaqtulu	3rd MASCULINE	*y/taqtulūna*
taqtulu	3rd FEMININE	*taqtulna*
taqtulu	2nd MASCULINE	*taqtulūna*
taqtulīna	2nd FEMININE	*taqtulna*
ʾaqtulu	1st COMMON	*naqtulu*

DUAL	
3rd COMMON	*y/taqtulāni*
2nd COMMON	*taqtulāni*
1st COMMON	*naqtulāni*

Variations

Ugaritic (or our understanding of it) is not always as precise as we would like it to be. For example, sometimes, for no apparent reason, the *-na* at the end of the form for the 2fs, 2mp, and 3mp is not written. Similarly, sometimes the *-ni* at the end of the form for the duals is not written either.

Patterns

Normally, the second vowel (the theme vowel) of the verb form is a *u* (or *i*) and the preformative vowel is an *a*. However, if the second or third root letter is a guttural, then the theme vowel is an *a* and the preformative vowel is an *i*. If the initial or final root letter is a *y*, then the theme vowel is an *i*.

Examples: *paʿnêhu lêhadāmi yaṯpudu*	His feet on the footstool he sets.
wayiṣḥaqu	And he laughs.
yišlaḥu ḫurāṣa	He beats out gold.
biyaʿri yahdiyu	With a razor he cuts.

Use

Agreement

Verbs will usually agree in gender and number with their subjects. The operative word here is *usually*.

Examples:	*šamûma šamna tamṭurūna*	The heavens rain oil.
	qudšu yiʾḫadu mušabʿira	Qudšu grasps a torch.

Location

Ugaritic is somewhat flexible in its placement of the verb in a sentence.

Examples:	*bisiʾni lapūši tašaṣîqannahu*	By the hem of the garment, she seizes him.
	laʾû šamûma biyadi môti	The heavens stood still because of Môt.
	šamûma šamna tamṭurūna	The heavens rain oil.

Exercises

Vocalize the following Ugaritic words. Parse and translate the verbs. Some forms will have more than one possible correct answer. Use the glossary at the back of the book to help you with any unfamiliar words.

1. *ypʿr* Vocalization:

Parsing:

TENSE	PERSON	GENDER	NUMBER

Translation:

2. *an bnt* Vocalization:

Parsing:

TENSE	PERSON	GENDER	NUMBER

Translation:

3. *at tmḫṣ* Vocalization:

Parsing:

TENSE	PERSON	GENDER	NUMBER

Translation:

4. *qritm* Vocalization:

Parsing:

TENSE	PERSON	GENDER	NUMBER

Translation:

5. *amlk* Vocalization:

Parsing:

TENSE	PERSON	GENDER	NUMBER

Translation:

6. *hw ymlu* Vocalization:

Parsing:

TENSE	PERSON	GENDER	NUMBER

Translation:

7. *atm tlḥmn* Vocalization:

Parsing:

TENSE	PERSON	GENDER	NUMBER

Translation:

8. *mǵny* Vocalization:

Parsing:

TENSE	PERSON	GENDER	NUMBER

Translation:

9. *at tṣmtn* Vocalization:

Parsing:

TENSE	PERSON	GENDER	NUMBER

Translation:

10. *hm yḫtan* Vocalization:

Parsing:

TENSE	PERSON	GENDER	NUMBER

Translation:

For Further Study

Dobrusin, Deborah L. "The Third Masculine Plural of the Prefixed Form of the Verb in Ugaritic." *Journal of the Ancient Near Eastern Society* 13 (1981): 5–14.

Argues that the 3mp *yaqtulu* form was formed with a prefixed *t* and not *y*. Gives examples and discusses disputed forms.

Fenton, Terry L. "Command and Fulfillment in Ugaritic—'TQTL: YQTL' and 'QTL: QTL.'" *Journal of Semitic Studies* 14 (1969): 34–38.

Compares two ways a command and its fulfillment are narrated and discusses why a writer might have chosen either of these ways.

Greenstein, Edward L. "Forms and Functions of the Finite Verb in Ugaritic Narrative Verse." Pages 75–102 in *Biblical Hebrew in Its Northwest Semitic Setting: Typological and Historical Perspectives*. Edited by Steven E. Fassberg and Avi Hurvitz. Winona Lake, Ind.: Eisenbrauns, 2006.

Argues that the variation of QTL and YQTL in Ugaritic poetry is not due to differences of tense or aspect.

———. "On a New Grammar of Ugaritic" (review of Daniel Sivan, *A Grammar of the Ugaritic Language*). Pages 397–420 in *Past Links: Studies in the Languages and Cultures of the Ancient Near East*. Israel Oriental Studies 18. Edited by Shlomo Isre'el, Itamar Singer, and Ran Zadok. Winona Lake, Ind.: Eisenbrauns, 1998.

Overall, a positive review of Sivan's grammar. See page 408 for a discussion of the 3mp *yaqtulu* form. Pages 409–413 dispute the existence of the shorter *yaqtul* form.

Sivan, Daniel. "The Use of *QTL* and *YQTL* Forms in the Ugaritic Verbal System." Pages 89–103 in *Past Links: Studies in the Languages and Cultures of the Ancient Near East*. Israel Oriental Studies 18. Edited by Shlomo Isre'el, Itamar Singer, and Ran Zadok. Winona Lake, Ind.: Eisenbrauns, 1998.

Clear summary and examples of the functions of *QTL* and *YQTL* forms. Includes discussions of tense and aspect as well as the short *yaqtul* form. Very helpful.

Tropper, Josef. "Das ugaritische Verbalsystem: Bestandaufnahme der Formen und statistische Auswertung." *Ugarit-Forschungen* 24 (1992): 313–37.

Includes a twenty-two-page list that is accessible without knowledge of German. Categorizes every verbal form in much of *KTU* according to conjugation and mood.

LESSON 8: MOODS

This term refers to those forms of the verb that communicate specific nuances regarding the disposition (or mood) of the speaker. The moods are the indicative, energic, jussive, subjunctive (volitive-*a*), and imperative.

Indicative

Meaning

The indicative mood communicates the nuance of simple statement or assertion. It is the basic meaning of the *yaqtulu* conjugation.

Form

The form of the indicative is the form of the *yaqtulu* that you have already learned. Yes, that's right; there is nothing new for you to learn here.

Energic

Meaning

The energic mood communicates the nuance of energy (hence, energ-ic), force, vigor, or power. In contemporary English, this is communicated by means of an auxiliary word such as "really" preceding the verb, as in "I really hit my knee on the stairs."

Form

In the energic mood, all of the *yaqtulu* forms that end with *-u* (3ms, 3fs, 2ms, 1cs, 1cp) replace the *-u* with *-anna*. If the verb has a pronominal suffix, the *-anna* will occur before the pronominal suffix (as below).

Examples: *biʾiššati tašrup**anna**nu* With fire she (really) burns him
*bišadī tidraʿ**anna**nu* In the field she (really) sows him

Notice how what would have been *tašrupunu* and *tidraʿunu* in the indicative mood in the two examples above have been changed to the energic mood by replacing the *-u-* before the 3ms pronominal suffix (*-nu*) with *-anna-*.

Jussive (Volitive-Ø)

Meaning

The jussive mood expresses a command, order, or exhortation (i.e., an action relating to the will or *volition*) usually, but not always, in the third person. In contemporary English, this is communicated by means of words such as "let him...," "let her...," "let it...," or "let them...," as in "Let them eat cake!"

Form

In the jussive mood, all of the *-u* endings of the *yaqtulu* forms are dropped (hence the name "Volitive-Ø," meaning *volative with no ending*) and all the *-na* and *-ni* endings are dropped except those of the 2fp and 3fp forms. The following table gives the basic forms for *hlm* (to strike).

PERSON/GENDER	SINGULAR	DUAL	PLURAL
3rd MASCULINE	*yahlum*	*y/tahlumā*	*y/tahlumū*
3rd FEMININE	*tahlum*	*tahlumā*	*tahlumna*
2nd MASCULINE	*tahlum*	*tahlumā*	*tahlumū*
2nd FEMININE	*tahlumī*		*tahlumna*
1st COMMON	*ʾahlum*	*nahlumā*	*nahlum*

Examples: *yaʾkulū* Let them eat! (3mp from *ʾkl*)
yaʿmus Let him construct! (3ms from *ʿms*)

A negative command, or prohibition, is indicated by using the negator *ʾal* before the 2nd person form of the jussive.

Examples: *ʾal taqrubā* Do not draw near! (2md from *qrb*)
ʾal tappulā Do not fall! (2cd from *npl*)

Volitive-*a*

Meaning

There is another proposed volitional mood of uncertain relationship to the jussive that, it is suggested, communicates the nuance of contingency or hypotheticality. In contemporary English, this nuance is communicated by means of words such as "would," "could," "should," "might," or "may" preceding the verb, as in "He might enter the Ph.D. program."

Form

In this volitional mood, sometimes called the subjunctive, all of the *yaqtulu* forms that end with *-u* (3ms, 3fs, 2ms, 1cs, 1cp) replace the *-u* with *-a* (hence the name "Volitive-*a*"); the *-na* ending of the 2fs, 2mp, and 3mp is dropped; and the *-ni* ending of the dual forms is dropped. At least this is the proposed form. The actual existence of this volitional mood is not entirely certain due to the limitations of what we can observe in the consonantal text.

Imperative

Meaning

The imperative mood expresses a command, order, or exhortation in the second person. The "you" (singular or plural) is not expressed. For example, "Sit down!" employs an imperative.

Form

The imperative mood is formed by removing the preformative elements (that is, the initial consonant and vowel) from the second person *yaqtulu* forms (minus the final vowel and any *-na* or *-ni* endings). Because the imperative form is based on the *yaqtulu* form, the patterns governing the theme vowel of the *yaqtulu* (discussed on p. 64 above) also apply to the imperative. The following table gives the basic forms for *hlm* (to strike).

MASCULINE SINGULAR	*h(u)lum(a)*
FEMININE SINGULAR	*h(u)lumī*
MASCULINE PLURAL	*h(u)lumū*
FEMININE PLURAL	*h(u)lumā(?)*
DUAL	*h(u)lumā*

The first vowel (the one in parentheses in the chart above) may not be present if the form is preceded by a vowel (see the third example below). If the first vowel must be supplied, it is simply the same vowel as the theme vowel.

The feminine plural form has a question mark following it in the chart above because this form is only speculated based on other languages.

As in Hebrew, an *-a* may be attached to the end of the masculine singular form, with no obvious effect on the meaning.

Imperatives may also be followed by the particle *mʿ* (*maʿ*). This particle does not seem to affect the meaning in an obvious way.

Examples:	*šamaʿī*	Hear! (fs from *šmʿ*)
	šamaʿ maʿ	Hear! (ms from *šmʿ*)
	qaraʾa	Call! (ms from *qrʾ* with final *a*)
	huburū	Bow down! (mp from *hbr*)
	wargumū	And say! (mp from *rgm*)

Remember, the imperative form is not used to indicate a negative command, or prohibition. Rather, as in Hebrew, a negative command is indicated by using the negator *ʾal* before the 2nd person form of the jussive (see p. 70 above).

Exercises

Vocalize and translate the following Ugaritic words. Parse the verb forms. Some forms will have more than one possible correct answer. For the definitions of unfamiliar words, consult the vocabulary list at the back of the book.

1. *šmʿ lbtlt ʿnt*

Parsing:

MOOD	PERSON	GENDER	NUMBER

Translation:

2. *mh taršn*

Parsing:

MOOD	PERSON	GENDER	NUMBER

Translation:

3. *tlḥm rpum*

Parsing:

MOOD	PERSON	GENDER	NUMBER

Translation:

4. *ltikl* (The initial *l* is vocalized as *lā*—see vocabulary list. Also, regarding the *i*, remember the discussion regarding the consonant ʾ in Lesson 2: Language Basics)

Parsing:

MOOD	PERSON	GENDER	NUMBER

Translation:

5. *ym ymm yʿtqn*

Parsing:

MOOD	PERSON	GENDER	NUMBER

Translation:

6. *lḥm bṯlḥnt*

Parsing:

MOOD	PERSON	GENDER	NUMBER

Translation:

7. *lpʿn mt hbr*

Parsing:

MOOD	PERSON	GENDER	NUMBER

Translation:

8. *šmm šmn tmṭrn*

Parsing:

MOOD	PERSON	GENDER	NUMBER

Translation:

9. *al tqrb*

Parsing:

MOOD	PERSON	GENDER	NUMBER

Translation:

10. ***bḥrb tbqʿnn***

Parsing:

MOOD	PERSON	GENDER	NUMBER

Translation:

For Further Study

Krebernik, Manfred. "Verbalformen mit suffigierten n-Morphemen im Ugaritischen: Überlegungen zur Morphologie des Energikus im Ugaritischen und in anderen semitischen Sprachen." Pages 125–50 in *Syntax und Text: Beiträge zur 22. Internationalen Ökumenischen Hebräisch-Dozenten-Konferenz 1993 in Bamberg*. Edited by Hubert Irsigler. Arbeiten zu Text und Sprache im Alten Testament 40. St. Ottilien: EOS, 1993.

Includes an eleven-page chart that is accessible without any knowledge of German. It lists, parses, and cites verbal forms that occur with a suffixed *n*.

Moran, William L. "Early Canaanite *yaqtula*." *Orientalia* 29 (1960): 1–19.

Assumes knowledge of Akkadian—all passages from the Amarna letters.

Rainey, Anson F. "The Prefix Conjugation Patterns of Early Northwest Semitic." Pages 407–20 in *Lingering Over Words: Studies in Ancient Near Eastern Literature in Honor of William L. Moran*. Harvard Semitic Studies 37. Edited by Tzvi Abusch et al. Atlanta: Scholars Press, 1990.

Complicated to understand without knowledge of other Semitic languages. Very detailed.

———. "Is There Really a *yaqtula* Conjugation Pattern in the Canaanite Amarna Tablets?" *Journal of Cuneiform Studies* 43–45 (1991–93): 107–18.

Assumes knowledge of Akkadian.

Richardson, Mervyn E. J. "Tense, Aspect, and Mood in Ugaritic YQTL." Pages 283–89 in vol. 2 of *Proceedings of the Fifth International Hamito-Semitic Congress 1987*. 2 vols. Edited by Hans G. Mukarovsky. Veröffentlichungen der Institute für Afrikanistik und Ägyptologie der Universität Wien 56. Beiträge zur Afrikanistik 40–41. Vienna: Afro-Pub, 1991.

LESSON 9: INFINITIVES

Infinitive Construct

Explanation

The infinitive construct is peculiar in that it is a verbal noun. That is, it behaves like a noun and also like a verb. The closest approximation to it in English is the gerund. This piece of information might not help you very much without some further explanation. In English, a gerund is a noun that ends in *-ing*. For example the noun subject in the sentence "Food is forbidden" can be replaced by the gerund/infinitive construct *smoking*: "Smoking is forbidden." Both *food* and *smoking* are nouns functioning the same way in the sentence. However, because *smoking* is a *verbal* noun, it may also take a direct object: "Smoking cigarettes is forbidden."

Example: *halāku baᶜli* the coming of Baᶜal

The infinitive construct may also be translated like the infinitive in English; that is, it may have the word "to" preceding a basic form of the verb. For example, "to eat," "to drink," and "to be merry" are all infinitives. This is only a slight variation from what was discussed in the first paragraph. For example, "Smoking is forbidden" means the same thing as "To smoke is forbidden," and "Smoking cigarettes is forbidden" means the same thing as "To smoke cigarettes is forbidden."

Example: *maḫāṣu binīya* to slay my sons

Inflection

The infinitive construct does not have endings for number or gender, but it does have an ending for case. Thus, the basic form for the infinitive construct (using the root *qtl*) is: *qatāl-* (*u/i/a*). Of course, like all nouns (it is, after all, a *verbal* noun), the infinitive construct may have a *-ma* attached at the end.

Example: *qatāluma*

Uses

1. Temporal Clause

The inseparable preposition *bi-* attached to the beginning of the infinitive construct creates a temporal clause.

Example: *binašāʾi ʿênêha* — upon lifting (= in the lifting of, when she lifted) her eyes

2. Purpose Clause

The inseparable preposition *lê-* attached to the beginning of the infinitive construct creates a purpose clause

Example: *yaṯabū binū qudši lêṯarāmi* — the sons of holiness had sat down to dine

3. Gerundive or Infinitive Use

The infinitive construct also has its normal gerundive or infinitive use as seen in the examples provided above under "Explanation."

Infinitive Absolute

Explanation

The infinitive absolute has an adverbial force; it usually modifies the verb in some way (although for other applications, see below). In accomplishing this function, it comes immediately before the verb it is modifying.

Inflection

None. The basic form (using the root *qtl*) is *qatālu.* To this basic form is often added a final *-ma*, which has no apparent effect on the meaning.

Uses

1. To add emphasis to the verb

The infinitive absolute may be placed *before* a verb of the same three-letter root to add emphasis to the verb.

Example: *raǵābu raǵabti* — Are you ***very*** hungry?
ǵamāʾu ǵamiʾti — Are you ***very*** thirsty?

The infinitive absolute may be placed *after* a verb of the same or different three-letter root to draw out or explain the action of the verb.

Example: *tiṯʿaru kussīʾāti lêmāhirī*
ṯaʿāru ṯulḥanāti lêṣabaʾīma
She *throws* chairs at the professionals,
throwing tables at the soldiers.

2. To stand for a regular verb (finite preterit)

It is possible that the infinitive absolute is sometimes used in place of a regular verb. Where this possibility is present, it seems to be a matter of convenience. It is often proposed that the infinitive absolute at times takes the place of an imperative or a regular past-tense verb.

As an Imperative:

Though most grammars suggest this use for the infinitive absolute, unambiguous examples are nonexistent.

As a Regular Verb:

It is also difficult to provide certain examples of this use of the infinitive absolute because the forms lack vowels. One may therefore always argue that we are dealing with a regular verb or a participle instead of an infinitive absolute. Nevertheless, the following are provided as clear examples (because Anat is feminine and neither *šmḫ* nor *ṣḥq* has a feminine form, as they would have to if they were regular verbs).

Example:	*šamāḫu batūlatu ᶜanatu*	The virgin Anat rejoiced.
	ṣaḥāqu batūlatu ᶜanatu	The virgin Anat laughed.

Exercises

Using the glossary provided in the back of the book, provide the correct vocalization and translation for the Ugaritic words found in the following sentences and phrases. Because you have no context, there may be more than one correct vocalization/translation for these sentences and phrases. Underline the infinitive constructs and infinitive absolutes.

1. Have you come *mḫṣy hm mḫṣ bny*?

2. *byṣi nšm*

3. *llḥm wlšty ṣḥtkm*

4. *mzl ymzl*?

5. *tbᶜ ank*

6. *ydʿ lydʿt*

7. *wyqrb bšal krt*

8. *šmʿ ilt*

For Further Study

Gai, Amikam. "The Reduction of the Tense (and Other Categories) of the Consequent Verb in North-West Semitic." *Orientalia* 51 (1982): 254–56.

Examples of infinitives standing for regular verbs in Ugaritic, Biblical Hebrew, and Phoenician.

Marcus, David. "Studies in Ugaritic Grammar 1." *Journal of the Ancient Near Eastern Society of Columbia University* 1/2 (1969): 55–61.

Argues that infinitive absolutes did not stand for regular verbs indicating past time.

Moran, William L. "The Use of the Canaanite Infinitive Absolute as a Finite Verb in the Amarna Letters from Byblos." *Journal of Cuneiform Studies* 4 (1950): 169–72.

Assumes an understanding of Akkadian.

LESSON 10: THEMATIC STEMS

A "thematic" stem is a major inflectional category of a verb that gives its own particular nuance to the verbal action. That explanation might need explanation! A thematic stem is a particular modification to the three-letter root of a Semitic verb. The three-letter root has its own basic meaning, but the thematic stem, represented by a specific pattern of vowels and/or consonants added to the three-letter root, tweaks that express meaning in a recognizable and fairly consistent way. The specific patterns and their nuances are discussed below.

G Stem

Meaning

The G stem is the ground (that's where the "G" comes from) or basic stem that all the other stems modify in order to add their particular nuance. Everything we've learned about the verbs so far has been for the G stem.

Characteristics

No special characteristics beyond those already discussed.

Gt Stem

Meaning

This modification of the basic stem signifies a reflexive sense; that is, the subject performs the basic meaning of the G stem to itself. For example, if a G stem verb means "I cut (something)," in the Gt stem it would mean "I cut myself." Because Gt stem verbs have this reflexive nuance, they do not usually take a direct object. The subject of the verb is, in effect, the direct object.

Characteristics

1. A *-t-* is inserted (that is, "infixed") after the first root letter of the verb.

2. In the *qatala* conjugation, the pattern is:
   ʾi①ta②i③ + appropriate verb ending (where ①②③ are the three root consonants)
   Note the infixed *-t-* between the first and second root letters.

   Example: *šʾr* — 3ms G QTL: *šaʾira* He left (something over)
   3ms Gt QTL: *ʾištaʾira* It remained

3. In the *yaqtulu* conjugation, the pattern is:
   preformative consonant + *i①ta②i③* + appropriate verb ending

   Example: *rḥṣ* — 3ms G YQTL: *yirḥaṣu yadêhu* He washes his hands
   3ms Gt YQTL: *yirtaḥiṣu* He washes himself

4. The imperative drops the preformative consonant and vowel of the *yqtl* and we would therefore be left with a word beginning with two consonants (a big no-no in Semitic languages). The problem is solved by adding an *i* vowel at the beginning (called a "prothetic" vowel— a fancy word meaning it's placed at the beginning). Of course, it doesn't need to do this if it already has a vowel in front of it (due to a conjunction, for example).

   Examples: *ʾištamiʿ* Hear! (ms)
   waštamiʿ And hear! (ms)

N Stem

Meaning

This modification of the basic stem signifies a passive or reflexive sense; that is, the basic meaning of the G stem is done to the subject of the verb by an unnamed entity (passive) or the subject performs the basic meaning of the G stem to itself (reflexive). For example, if a G stem verb means "I cut (something)," in the N stem it would mean either "I was cut" (by someone or something unnamed) or "I cut myself." Because N stem verbs have this passive or reflexive nuance, they do not usually take a direct object. The subject of the verb is, in effect, the direct object.

Characteristics

1. In the *qatala* (from here on, abbreviated to *qtl*) conjugation, the pattern is: *na①②a③* + appropriate verb ending
   Note the preformative *n-* that characterizes this verb stem

   Example: *lqḥ* — 3ms G QTL: *laqiḥa* He took
   3ms N QTL: *nalqaḥa* He was taken

2. In the *yaqtulu* (from here on, abbreviated to *yqtl*) conjugation, the pattern is:
   preformative consonant + *i*①①*a*②i③ + appropriate verb ending
   Note how the first consonant of the three-letter root is doubled because of the assimilated *n*. (See the discussion of Consonant Changes in Lesson 2, p. 33.)

   Example: *spr* — 2ms G YQTL: *taspuru* You will count
   2ms N YQTL: *tissapiru* You will be counted

3. The form and even the existence of the imperative is questioned.

4. The pattern for participle and infinitive is:
   *na*①②*a*③ + appropriate ending

D Stem

Meaning

The D stem is used for expressing those verbs that come from nouns or adjectives (that is, "denominative" verbs) or for expressing the idea of causing a state. For example, if a G stem verb means "I die," in the D stem it would mean "I cause to die" (that is, "I kill" or "I put [something or someone] into the state of death").

Characteristics

1. In the *qtl* conjugation, the pattern is:
   ①*a*②②*i*③ + appropriate verb ending

   Example: *ḫsr* — 3ms G QTL: *ḫasirtu* I was lacking
   3ms D QTL: *ḫassirtu* I took away (that is, I caused to be lacking)

2. In the *yqtl* conjugation, the pattern is:
   preformative consonant + *a*①*a*②②*i*③ + appropriate verb ending

   Examples: *talabbinu* You will make bricks (from *lbn*)
   yanaḥḥitu He brings down (from *nḥt*)

3. The imperative drops the preformative consonant of the second person *yaqtulu* forms (as well as final vowels and any *-na* or *-ni* endings).

   Example: *kabbidā* Honor! (masculine dual from *kbd*)

4. The participle pattern is: *mu*①*a*②②*i*③+ appropriate ending

Example: *muʿammisuha* He is carrying her (from *ʿms*)

5. The infinitive pattern is: ①*u*②②*a*③+ appropriate ending

Example: *pullaṭu* to deliver (from *plṭ*)

tD Stem

Meaning

This rarely occurring verb stem is the reflexive of the D stem.

Characteristics

This verb stem inserts ("infixes") a *-ta-* before the first letter of the three-letter root. It then follows the same pattern as the D stem.

Example: *tabaššir* Be informed! (ms imperative from *bšr*)
Note: In this case, the *ta*- that begins this imperative form is the *ta*- of the tD stem. The 3fs *yqtl* D Stem form is very similar: *tabašširu*.

Š Stem

Meaning

The Š stem is the verb stem that is usually used to indicate that the subject of the verb is causing someone or something to perform the verbal action.

Characteristics

As you no doubt suspect, this verb stem is distinguished by the presence of a *š* (more precisely, a *ša*-) preceding the three-letter root in all forms.

Example: *ʾašaspiruka* I will cause you to count (1cs *yqtl* from *spr* + 2ms accusative pronominal suffix)

Št Stem

Meaning

The Št stem is the reflexive of the Š stem. That means that the subject of the verb causes itself to perform the verbal idea upon itself.

Characteristics

The Št stem inserts ("infixes") a *-t-* immediately after the *š*. The *š*, as we saw above, is located before the three-letter root.

Example: *tištaḥwiyu* She prostrates herself (3fs *yqtl* from *ḥwy*; that is, she causes herself to bow down)

R Stem

Meaning

The R stem performs the same function as the D stem for those verbs that have only two consonants.

Characteristics

The R stem gets its name from the fact that it doubles, or reduplicates (that's where the "R" comes from) the two strong consonants of the root.

Example: *yakarkiru ʾuṣbaʿātihu* He twiddles his fingers (3ms *yqtl* from from *kr*)

L Stem

Meaning

The L stem performs the same function as the D stem for middle-weak (verbs whose second letter is a *w* or a *y*) or geminate (verbs whose second and third root letters are the same) verbs.

Characteristics

This verb is charaterized by a long vowel (that's where the "L" comes from) after the first root letter in all its forms.

Examples: *yadu malki yaḫāsisuki* — The hand of the king excites you (3ms *yqtl* from *ḫss* + 2fs accusative pronominal suffix)

Summary of the Thematic Stems

The following chart gives the basic form of the root in each of the thematic stems. The forms are based on the root *qtl* where possible. The R and L stem forms necessarily require the use of a different root inasmuch as these stems are used for certain weak verbs, as described above. The blank boxes indicate unattested forms.

	Qtl	***Yqtl***	**IMPERATIVE**	**ACTIVE PARTICIPLE**	**PASSIVE PARTICIPLE**	**INFINITIVE**
G	*qatala*	*yaqtulu*	*q(u)tul*	*qātilu*	*qatūlu* *maqtūlu*	*qatālu*
Gt		*yiqtatilu*	*ʾiqtatil*			
N	*naqtala*	*yiqqatilu*		*naqtalu*		*naqtalu*
D	*qattila*	*yaqattilu*	*qattil*	*muqattilu*		*quttalu*
tD	*taqattala*	*yataqattilu*	*taqattil*			
Š	*šaqtila*	*yašaqtilu*	*šaqtil*	*mušaqtilu*		*šaqtalu*
Št		*yištaqtilu*				
R	*karkara*	*yakarkiru*				
L	*rāmama*	*yarāmimu*	*rāmim*	*murāmimu*		

Exercises

Using the vocabulary at the back of the book, identify and parse the verbs in the following passages, and then translate. "Root" is the three-letter root; "stem" is the thematic stem; and "aspect" is a shorthand term tense, mood, active or passive participle, infinitive construct or absolute.

1. *ʿanatu tanaggiṯuhu*

ROOT	**STEM**	**ASPECT or MOOD**	**PERSON/GENDER/NUMBER**

Translation:

2. *ʾahabtu ṯôri taʿāriruki*

ROOT	STEM	ASPECT or MOOD	PERSON/GENDER/NUMBER

Translation:

3. *šaskin maggāna*

ROOT	STEM	ASPECT or MOOD	PERSON/GENDER/NUMBER

Translation:

4. *ʾal tištaḥwiyā lêpuḫri môʿidi*

ROOT	STEM	ASPECT or MOOD	PERSON/GENDER/NUMBER

Translation:

5. *ʾarṣa darkati yištakinu*

ROOT	STEM	ASPECT or MOOD	PERSON/GENDER/NUMBER

Translation:

6. *kaʾimmari bipîhu tiḫḫatiʾāni*

ROOT	STEM	ASPECT or MOOD	PERSON/GENDER/NUMBER

Translation:

7. *dūyašabbiʿu hamullāti ʾarṣi*

ROOT	STEM	ASPECT or MOOD	PERSON/GENDER/NUMBER

Translation:

8. *ka'iššatêmi yi'tamirā*

ROOT	STEM	ASPECT or MOOD	PERSON/GENDER/NUMBER

Translation:

9. *yašattik ba'lu 'ênāti maḫrūṯāti*

ROOT	STEM	ASPECT or MOOD	PERSON/GENDER/NUMBER

Translation:

10. *yibbanî bêtu lêba'li*

ROOT	STEM	ASPECT or MOOD	PERSON/GENDER/NUMBER

Translation:

For Further Study

Krebernik, Manfred. "Gt- und tD-Stämme im Ugaritischen." Pages 227–70 in *Texte, Methode und Grammatik: Wolfgang Richter zum 65. Geburtstag*. Edited by Walter Gross, Hubert Irsigler, and Theodor Seidl. St. Ottilien: EOS, 1991.

Written in German, this chapter provides some helpful lists of Gt and tD verbs and where they occur in Ugaritic literature.

LESSON 11: WEAK VERBS

Weak verbs are those that do not have three strong consonants. What is a strong consonant, you ask? A strong consonant is one that does not combine with a vowel to form a diphthong (like *y* or *w*), sometimes disappear (like *h* or *n*), or assimilate (like ʾ or *n*). Instead, it stands its ground in the face of swirling grammatical changes all around. The world would be a nicer place if every consonant were strong. However, in this fallen world we must deal with the presence of weak consonants and compensate for their peculiarities by making certain "adjustments" to the normal paradigms we have learned so far.

Initial-*n* Verbs

Initial-*n* verbs are those whose first root letter is an *n*.

Peculiarities

1. Remember, the *n* is a sociable consonant that likes to assimilate into (that is, become the same as) whatever consonant follows it. So, if we follow the normal verb paradigms and end up with a form in which the *n* is right next to another consonant with no vowel in between, the *n* will assimilate into that consonant.

   Examples: G YQTL 3ms of *npl* — *yappulu* He falls
   We expect *yanpulu*, but the *n* has assimilated into the *p* (resulting in *pp*).
   G YQTL 3ms of *nšʾ* — *yiššaʾu ʿênêhu* He lifts his eyes
   We expect *yinšaʾu*, but the *n* has assimilated into the *š* (resulting in *šš*).

2. The *n* is absent in the G stem imperative (just as it is in Hebrew).

   Example: G Imperative fs of *nšʾ* — *šaʾī ʿênêki* Lift your eyes!
   Notice how the *n* disappears from the beginning of the form.

3. When the *n* is present in the transliteration, it means that it has not assimilated and is therefore followed by a vowel.

   Example: *wynšq* *wayanaššiqu* and he kisses
   Note: Because the *n* is present, the verb cannot be a G stem. If it were, the *n* would have assimilated (*wayanšuqu* would

go to *wayaššuqu*) and not be written in the consonantal transliteration. Because the *n* is present, the verb stem must be one in which a vowel follows the *n* (such as the D stem here).

LQḤ

This verb is listed here after the discussion of initial-*n* verbs because it mistakenly believes it is one. We know it really isn't an initial-*n* verb, but we'll play along to keep it happy.

Peculiarities

1. The *l* assimilates as though it were an *n*.

   Example: G YQTL 3ms — *yiqqaḥu* He takes
   We expect *yilqaḥu*, but the *l* has assimilated into the *q* as if it were an *n*.

2. As in initial-*n* verbs, the *l* is absent in the G stem imperative.

   Example: G Imperative ms — *qaḥ* Take!

Final-*n* Verbs

Final-*n* verbs are those whose final root letter is an *n*.

Peculiarities

Unexpectedly, when the *n* occurs in this position of the verb, it is not assimilated into a following consonant. Go figure.

Example: G QTL 2ms from *ytn* — *yatanta* You gave

Initial-ʾ Verbs

Initial-ʾ verbs are those whose first root letter is an ʾ.

Peculiarities

1. In the G stem, the ʾ is usually retained.

Example: G Imperative ms from *ʾrš* — *ʾuruš* Ask!
G YQTL 3fs from *ʾḫd* — *tiʾḫadu* She grabs

2. In the Gt stem, the ʾ sometimes assimilates to the infixed *-t-*.

Example: Gt YQTL 3ms from *ʾmr* — *yittamiru* He sees
We expect *yiʾtamiru*, but the ʾ has assimilated into the *t*.

However, this assimilation does not always occur. The form *yitmr* occurs, which implies that the ʾ is still present (that is, ***yiʾtamiru***).

Initial-*y/w* Verbs

This category combines verbs beginning with either of these consonants because initial-***w*** verbs have almost all shifted to initial-***y***. However, when the ***w*** does not begin the word, it is sometimes retained. For example, ***wayawassirū*** ("and they instruct") is the D stem, *yqtl* form (minus the ***-na*** at the end) of the three-letter root normally written elsewhere as ***ysr*** (but here, obviously, appears as ***wsr***).

Peculiarities

1. The initial root letter disappears in the G stem *yqtl* conjugation.

Examples: G YQTL 1cs from *ytn* — *ʾatinu* I shall give
G YQTL 1cs from *ybl* — *ʾabilu* I shall bring
G YQTL 3fs from *yld* — *talidu* She bears

2. The G stem 3ms *qtl*, 3ms *yqtl*, and ms participle appear identical. For example, ***ybl*** could be vocalized as ***yabala*** (he brought), or ***yabilu*** (he will bring), or ***yābilu*** (bringing). As usual, we are dependent on the context to make the correct determination, although this sometimes does not entirely remove ambiguities.

3. The first root letter disappears in the G stem imperative.

Examples: G Imperative ms from *ytn* — *tin* Give!
G Imperative ms from *yṯb* — *ṯib* Sit!

4. In the Gt stem, the initial-*y/w* assimilates to the infixed *-t-*.

Example: Gt YQTL from *yrṯ* — *ʾittariṯu* I shall get for myself
Where we would expect *ʾiytariṯu*

5. In the Š stem, the initial-*y/w* combines with adjacent vowels to form *ô*.

Examples: Š QTL 3ms from *yṣʾ* — *šôṣaʾa* He brought out
Š YQTL 3ms from *yṣʾ* — *yašôṣiʾu* He will bring out

HLK

This verb is listed here after the discussion of initial-*y/w* verbs because it mistakenly believes it is one. We know it really isn't an initial-*y/w* verb, but we'll play along to keep it happy.

Peculiarities

1. The *h* disappears in the G stem *yqtl* conjugation.

Example: *taliku* She walks

2. In the Gt stem, the *h* assimilates to the infixed *-t-*.

Example: *tittaliku* She walks around

3. The *h* disappears in the G stem imperative.

Example: *likā* Walk! (fp or dual)

Hollow Verbs

Hollow verbs are the OREO® cookie verbs of Ugaritic grammar. They have hard outer consonant shells, with creamy vowel middles. Technically, their middle consonants (*y* or *w*) have combined with vowels to become diphthongs.

Peculiarities

1. In the G *qtl* conjugation, the middle vowel (also called the theme vowel) is a long *ā* when no consonant immediately follows the last root consonant, and a short *a* when one does. This pattern holds no matter what the original middle vowel of the root is.

Examples: *bāʾat* (G QTL 3fs from *bwʾ*; middle *a* vowel) She came
wašatta (G QTL 2ms from *šyt*; middle *i* vowel) And you placed
naḫtu (G QTL 1cs from *nwḫ*; middle *u* vowel) I rested

2. In the G *yqtl* conjugation, the original middle vowel of the root is visible.

Examples:	*taqûmu*	(G YQTL 3fs from *qwm)*	She rises
	tadînu	(G YQTL 2ms from *dyn*)	You judge

3. In the G infinitive construct, the original middle vowel of the root is visible.

Example: *biʿûpi* (from *ʿwp*) in flight

4. Because the middle vowels of these verbs do not show up in the consonantal text, the G stem imperative, infinitive construct, ms participle, and 3ms *qtl* forms appear identical. We are entirely dependent upon context to help us make distinctions. However, context does not always completely resolve amibiguities.

Example: *št* could be:

šît	Place...! (ms imperative)
šîtī	Place...! (fs imperative)
šîtū	Place...! (mp imperative)
šîtā	Place...! (fp imperative)
šîtu	to place (infinitive construct)
šāta	He placed (3ms *qtl*)
šātu	placing (ms participle)

Final-*y* Verbs

Final-*y* verbs are those whose final root letter is a *y*.

Peculiarities

1. The general rule for these verbs is this: If the *y* is followed by a vowel, it is written in the consonantal text. If the *y* is not followed by a vowel, it will combine with the vowel that precedes it to form a diphthong and, therefore, will not be represented in the consonantal text (because it's not acting like a consonant anymore).

Examples:	*pdy* — *padaya*	He redeemed (G QTL 3ms)
	wyʿny — *wayaʿniyu*	And he answers (G YQTL 3ms)
	bny — *bāniyu*	Creator (G active participle ms)

In these cases, the *y* is followed by a vowel and so appears in the consonantal text.

štt — *šatêtu* I drank (G QTL 1cs from *šty*)
ˁl — *ˁilî* Arise! (G imperative ms from *ˁly*)
In these cases, the *y* is not followed by a vowel and so it combines with the preceding vowel to form a diphthong and does not appear in the consonantal text.

2. Of course, things don't always work this smoothly. Sometimes a verb or verbal form will omit the final vowel, even though the paradigm does not call for this to happen. When it does this to a final-*y* verb, the *y* will still combine with the preceding vowel to form a diphthong. Another explanation, or perhaps a separate phenomenon, is that the vowel preceding the *y*, the *y*, and the vowel following the *y* all combine to form a triphthong. Yikes! Usually in these cases, the final vowel of the triphthong is the one that wins out.

Examples: *bbk* — *babakî* in weeping (G infinitive construct from *bky*)
We would expect *babakāyi*

yˁl — *yaˁlû* He goes up (G YQTL 3ms from *ˁly*)
We would expect *yaˁliyu*

Geminate Verbs

Geminate verbs are verbs whose second and third root letters are the same. Happily, there are only a few.

Peculiarities

1. In the G *qtl* conjugation, there appears to be two basic formations. In one, the geminate verb behaves normally. In the other, the geminate verb behaves almost like a hollow verb, with the second and third root letters acting together as a single letter.

Examples: *nṭṭt* — *naṭaṭat* She leaped (G QTL 3fs from *nṭṭ*)
In this case, the verb is behaving normally.

sb — *sabba* It turned (G QTL 3ms from *sbb*)
In this case, the verb acts similarly to a hollow verb.

2. In the G *yqtl* conjugation, there also appear to be two basic formations. In one, the geminate verb behaves normally. In the other, the geminate verb behaves almost like a hollow verb, with the second and third root letters acting together as a single letter.

Examples: *ṭl yṭll* — *ṭallu yaṭlulu* The dew falls (G YQTL 3ms from *ṭll*)
In this case, the verb is behaving normally.

ygz — *yaguzzu* He will shear (G YQTL 3ms from *gzz*)
In this case, the verb acts similarly to a hollow verb.

Doubly Weak Verbs

For these verbs, two of the three root letters are weak consonants. The most common of these is *ḥwy*, particularly in the Št stem.

Example: *tištaḥwiyu* She prostrates herself

Exercises

Provide the vowels, three-letter root, and translation for the following weak verb forms. Use the glossary at the back of the book to help you with any unfamiliar vocabulary.

1. *tiḫd* (G, YQTL, 3fs)

2. *tššqnh* (Š, YQTL, 3fs + energic and 3ms object suffix)

3. *tlk* (G, YQTL, 3fs)

4. *idᶜ* (G, YQTL, 1cs)

5. *aṯbn* (G, YQTL, 1cs + energic)

6. *yštk* (Š, Jussive, 3ms)

7. *pl* (G, QTL, 3mp)

8. *knyt* (G, Passive Participle, fp)

9. *nḫt* (G, Active Participle, fs)

10. *tʿn* (G, YQTL, 3fs)

For Further Study

General Works

Sivan, Daniel. "Final Triphthongs and Final Yu/a/i - Wu/a/i Diphthongs in Ugaritic Nominal Forms," *Ugarit-Forschungen* 14 (1982): 209–18.

Argues that there is no way to predict whether these types of diphthongs and triphthongs would or would not contract.

———. "Diphthongs and Triphthongs in Verbal Forms of Verba Tertiae in Ugaritic." *Ugarit-Forschungen* 16 (1984): 279–93.

Explores the behavior of *y* and *w* in verbal forms and how diphthongs may or may not contract. Includes many examples with translations.

First-ʾ

Greenstein, Edward L. "On a New Grammar of Ugaritic" (review of Daniel Sivan, *A Grammar of the Ugaritic Language*). Pages 397–420 in *Past Links: Studies in the Languages and Cultures of the Ancient Near East.* Israel Oriental Studies 18. Edited by Shlomo Isre'el, Itamar Singer, and Ran Zadok. Winona Lake, Ind.: Eisenbrauns, 1998.

Overall, a positive review of Sivan's grammar. See pp. 407–8 for a note about *ʾi* closing a syllable on first- ʾ verbs.

Sivan, Daniel. "A Note on the Use of the *ʾu*-Sign in Ugaritic Roots with First *ʾaleph*." *Ugarit-Forschungen* 28 (1996): 554–59.

Discussion of the use of *ʾu* where a vowelless *ʾālep* is expected. Clear presentation of the problem and possible explanations.

First-*w/y/h*

Testen, David. "The I-*w* Verbal Class and the Reconstruction of the Early Semitic Preradical Vocalism." *Journal of the American Oriental Society* 114 (1994): 426–34.

Presumes understanding of other Semitic languages and grammar. Advanced.

Tsumura, David T. "The *Verba Prima WAW*, WLD, in Ugaritic." *Ugarit-Forschungen* 11 (1979): 779–82.

Argues for the existence of a verb with the three-letter root *wld* based on the examination of four passages in which it seems to appear.

Middle-ʾ*/w/y/h*

Segert, Stanislav. "Polarity of Vowels in the Ugaritic Verb II/ʾ/." *Ugarit-Forschungen* 15 (1983): 219–22.

Suggests that vowel polarity may be able to explain unexpected vowels in II-ʾ verb forms.

Geminates

Boyd, Jesse L. III. "The Development of the West Semitic Qal Perfect of the Double-ʿAyin Verb with Particular Reference to its Transmission into Syriac." *Journal of Northwest Semitic Languages* 10 (1982): 11–23.

Informative, but very complicated if one doesn't know Syriac or other Semitic languages and grammar.

Doubly Weak

Marcus, David. "The Verb 'To Live' in Ugaritic." *Journal of Semitic Studies* 17 (1972): 76–82.

Differentiates between the use of *ḥyy* in the G stem and *ḥwy* in the D stem.

LESSON 12: ADVERBS

Adverbs modify verbs, adjectives, and other adverbs. Let's look at some English examples.

An adverb modifying a verb: She learned ***quickly***.

Notice how "quickly" tells us something about *how* she learned.

An adverb modifying an adjective: She is ***very*** smart.

Notice how "very" tells us something about the adjective "smart."

An adverb modifying another adverb: She learned ***very*** quickly.

Notice how "quickly" is now modified by another adverb "very."

Adverbial Suffixes

-h (-ah)

1. Local

Example: *ʾarṣu* earth / *ʾarṣ**ah*** earthward

The *-ah* is also found attached to geographical and personal names.

2. Temporal

Example: *ʿālamu* time indefinite / *ʿālam**ah*** to eternity, forever

-m (-am)

This suffix makes a noun into an adverb. It has an effect similar to the suffix -ly in English.

Examples:	*gû*	voice	/	*gâm*	aloud, loudly
	bakāyu	weeping	/	*bakâm*	weepingly (while weeping)

Independent Adverbs

These adverbs do not attach directly to another word, but function as independent words in the sentence. While the following is not intended to be an exhaustive list, it does provide you with examples of some of the most common adverbs.

***aḫr* (*ʼaḫra*)** after, afterward

Example: ***ʾaḫra*** *maǵaya ʾalʾiyānu baʿlu* **Afterward** powerful Baʿal arrived

***al* (*ʼal*)**

1. Surely

Example: ***ʾal*** *tatinu pānīma* You will **surely** set your face....

2. Not (negates the jussive form to produce a prohibition)

Example: ***ʾal*** *targum laʾaḫātika* Do **not** tell your sister

***apnk* (*ʼappūnaka*)** then, thereupon

Example: ***ʾappūnaka*** *yaridu* **Then** he descends

***idk* (*ʼiddāka*)** then

Example: ***ʾiddāka*** *lūtatinu pānīma* **Then** she surely set [her] face...

***ht* (*hitta*)** now

Example: ***hitta*** *ʾêbaka timḫuṣu* **Now** your enemy you shall smite

***kn* (*kinna*)** thus

Example: ***kinna*** *napala baʿlu* **Thus** Baʿal fell

***mid* (*maʼda*)** very much

Example: *tabilūka ǵûrūma* ***maʾda*** *kaspa* The mountains will yield you **very much** silver

ṯamma there

Example: ***ṯamma*** *napala baʿlu* **There** Baʿal fell

Exercises

Vocalize and translate the Ugaritic words and phrases in the following passages. For the definitions of unfamiliar words, consult the vocabulary list at the back of the book.

1. *idk al ttn pnm ʿm ǵr*

2. *ht tṣmt ṣrtk*

3. *apnk alp yṭbḫ*

4. *mid tmtḫṣn*

5. *gm yṣḥ il*

6. *mǵy qrth*

7. *hlk ṯm*

8. *aḫr tmǵyn mlak ym*

For Further Study

Speiser, Ephraim A. "The Terminative-Adverbial in Canaanite-Ugaritic and Akkadian." *Israel Exploration Journal* 4 (1954): 108–15 = *Oriental and Biblical Studies*, 494–505.
Assumes knowledge of Akkadian and Semitic grammar.

LESSON 13: MISCELLANEA

How's that for a title? This section contains those stray grammatical elements that, like the platypus, don't really seem to belong to any fixed category, or belong to a category too small to warrant a whole lesson for each of them.

Conjunctions

Conjunctions simply connect words, phrases, or clauses. When they connect words, phrases, or clauses that are of equal significance, they are called ***coordinating*** conjunctions. When they connect words, phrases, or clauses that are dependent on or of secondary importance to other words, phrases, or clauses, they are called ***subordinating*** conjunctions.

Coordinating Conjunctions

1. ***w*** (***wa-***) and

Examples: *ʿittaliku* ***wa****ʾaṣîdu* — I have walked **and** hunted
ʿanatu ***waba****ʿlu* — Anat **and** Baʿal

2. ***p*** (***pa-***) and (frequently serves to connect sentences)

Example: ***pa****ʿabdu ʾanāku* — **And** am I a slave?

3. ***u*** (*ʾ****ô***) or

When this conjunction is attached to successive words, it means "either (this) or (that)" or "both (this) and (that)."

Example: *ʾ****ô****malku ʾ****ô****balmalku* — **Either** king **or** no-king

4. ***ap*** (*ʾ****ap***) also, moreover

Examples: *ʾ****ap*** *maṯnê rigmīma* — **Also** another matter
*ʾ****ap*** *ʾilūma laḥāmi yaṯabū* — **Moreover**, the gods sat down to eat.

Subordinating Conjunctions

1. ***aḫr*** (*ʾ****aḫra***) after

Example: *ʾ****aḫra*** *tamǵiyāni* — **After** they arrive

2. ***hlm*** (***halumma***) when, as soon as

Example: ***halumma*** *ʾilu yaphânnaha*	**As soon as** El sees her

3. ***hm*** (***himma***) if, or

Examples: ***himma*** *ḥayyu baʿlu*	**If** Baʿal is alive
laḥamī ***himma*** *štiyīma*	Eat **or** drink!

4. ***k*** (***kī***) because, when, if, that

Examples: ***kī*** *ḥayyu baʿlu*	**Because** Baʿal is alive
kī *ẖalaqa zabūlu*	**that** the prince had died

5. ***ʿd*** (***ʿadê***) up to, as far as, until

Example: ***ʿadê*** *tišbaʾu tamtaẖiṣu*	**Until** she is satisfied, she smites

Words Expressing Existence or Non-Existence

These words are not verbs in that they do not conjugate for person, number, or gender (although they may take pronominal suffixes having, of course, person, gender, and number). However they function in quasi-verbal manner to express being or lack of being.

Expressing Existence: *iṯ* (*ʾiṯê*)

Example: ***ʾiṯê*** *zabūlu baʿlu ʾarṣi*	The prince, the lord of the earth, **exists**

Expressing Non-existence: *in* (*ʾêna*)

Example: ***ʾêna*** *dūʿalênahu*	**There is not** one who is above him

Negators

As the name implies, negators are grammatical elements that negate things. Thus, they are usually translated as "not" or "no." Sometimes these negators are attached directly to the word they negate, and sometimes they stand alone.

1. ***l*** (***lā***) not

Example: *šiʾrahū* ***lā****taʾkulū ʿiṣṣūrūma*	Let the birds **not** eat his flesh!

2. ***al*** (*ʾ**al***) not (negation for a prohibition; used with the jussive)

Example: *ʾ**al** taqrubā*	Do **not** draw near!

3. ***bl*** (***bal***) no, without

Examples: *ʾômalku ʾô**bal**malku*	Either king or **no**-king
***bal** sipru*	**without** number

Interrogatives

Interrogatives introduce questions. They occur at the very beginning of the clause.

1. ***iy*** (*ʾ**êya***) where?

Example: *ʾ**êya** ʾalʾiyānu baʿlu*	**Where** is powerful Baʿal?

2. ***ik*** (*ʾ**êka***) why? how?

Example: *ʾ**êka** maǵayat*	**Why** has she arrived?

3. ***lm*** (***lêma***) why?

Example: ***lêma** ǵalêtum raʾšātikum*	**Why** did you lower your heads?

6. ***mh*** (***maha***) what?

Example: ***maha** taʾrušanna*	**What** do you want?

7. ***my*** (***mīya***) who?

Example: ***mīya** biʾilīma*	**Who** among the gods...?

Vocatives

"Vocative" is a term that describes the grammatical means used to indicate direct address or invocation. Hopefully, the following examples will provide clarification.

1. ***l-*** (***la-***)

Example: ***la**batūlatu ʿanatu*	**O** Virgin Anat!

2. ***y-*** (***yā-***)

Example: ***yā**šapšu*	**O** Šapšu!

Attention Grabbers

These grammatical elements correspond roughly to English words like "ahem," "hey," or "well." They are also known as interjections, presentation particles, or emphasizing particles. They are intended to grab the reader's or hearer's attention so that the weightiness of what follows is appreciated.

1. ***hl*** (***halā***) Look!

   Example: ***halā*** *ģalmatu talidu bina* — **Look**, the maiden bears a son!

2. ***hn*** (***hinnē***) Look!

   Example: ***wahinnē*** *ʾaṯṯatâmi taṣîḫāni* — And **look**, the two women shout

3. ***mk*** (***maka***) Behold!

   Example: ***maka*** *bašabʿi yômima* — **Behold**, on the seventh day. . .

4. ***k*** (***kī***) indeed, certainly

   Example: *baʿlu* ***kī*** *yaṣîḫu* — Baʿal **indeed** shouts!

5. ***l*** (***lū***) verily, surely

   Example: *lūḥakamta* — **Surely** you are wise

6. ***my*** (***maya***) Woe!

   Example: *maya liʾāmu* — **Woe**, O people!

Exercises

Vocalize and translate the Ugaritic words and phrases in the following passages. Use the glossary at the back of the book to help you with any unfamiliar words.

1. *ap ʿnt ttlk*

2. *šbt dqnk ltsrk*

3. *in bt lbʿl*

4. *wl yṯb*

5. *iy zbl bʿl arṣ*

6. *my hmlt*

7. *ʿd ilm ttlkn šd*

8. *lpʿn il al tpl*

For Further Study

Greenstein, Edward L. "On a New Grammar of Ugaritic" (review of Daniel Sivan, *A Grammar of the Ugaritic Language*). Pages 397–420 in *Past Links: Studies in the Languages and Cultures of the Ancient Near East.* Israel Oriental Studies 18. Edited by Shlomo Isre'el, Itamar Singer, and Ran Zadok. Winona Lake, Ind.: Eisenbrauns, 1998.

Overall, a positive review of Sivan's grammar. See pp. 413–14 for a brief clarification of Sivan's presentation of the vocative with prefix *l-*.

Singer, A. D. "The Vocative in Ugaritic." *Journal of Cuneiform Studies* II/1 (1948): 1–10.

Four ways to formulate direct address in Ugaritic and their occurrences.

Taylor, J. Glen. "A Long-Awaited Vocative Singular Noun with Final *Aleph* in Ugaritic (KTU 1.161.13)?" *Ugarit-Forschungen* 17 (1986): 315–18.

Response to Singer, 1948 (see above). Argues that a word in a specific passage that was previously identified as a genitive or accusative is more likely a vocative singular noun (previously unattested).

APPENDICES

SEMITIC CONSONANTS

The following chart shows how the Semitic consonants vary from one language to another. Ugaritic is in the left column as the base language to which the other Semitic consonants are being compared. This chart is useful for making or checking the legitimacy of comparisons between Ugaritic and other Semitic languages.

UGARITIC		HEBREW		ARAMAIC		ARABIC		AKKADIAN
ʾa	𐎀	ʾ	א	ʾ	א	ʾa	آ	ʾ[1]
ʾi	𐎛					ʾi	إ	
ʾu	𐎜					ʾu	أ	
b	𐎁	b	ב	b	ב	b	ب	b
g	𐎂	g	ג	g	ג	g	ج	g
d	𐎄	d/z	ד/ז	d/z	ד/ז	d	د	d/z
ḏ	𐎏	z	ז	d	ד	ḏ	ذ	z
h	𐎅	h	ה	h	ה	h	ه	ʾ[2]
w	𐎆	w/y	ו/י	w/y	ו/י	w	و	w/m/b
z	𐎇	z	ז	z	ז	z	ز	z
ḥ	𐎈	ḥ	ח	ḥ	ח	ḥ	ح	ʾ[3]
ḫ	𐎃	ḫ	ח	ḫ	ח	ḫ	خ	ḫ
ṭ	𐎉	ṭ	ט	ṭ	ט	ṭ	ط	ṭ
ẓ	𐎑	ṣ	צ	ṭ	ט	ẓ	ظ	ṣ
y	𐎊	y	י	y	י	y/w	و/ي	y/ʾ/w
k	𐎋	k	כ	k	כ	k	ك	k

l 𐎍	l ל	l ל	l ل	l
m 𐎎	m מ	m מ	m م	m
n 𐎐	n נ	n נ	n ن	n
s 𐎒	s/š שׁ/ס	s/ś שׂ/ס	s/š س	s/ś
s̀ 𐎝	s ס	š שׁ	š ش	š
ʿ 𐎓	ʿ ע	ʿ ע	ʿ ع	ʾ[4]
ġ 𐎙	ʿ/ṣ צ/ע	ʿ/ṭ ט/ע	ġ/ẓ ظ/غ	ʾ[5]/ṣ
p 𐎔	p פ	p פ	f ف	p
ṣ 𐎕	ṣ צ	ṣ/ʿ/q ק/ע/צ	ṣ/ḍ ض/ص	ṣ
q 𐎖	q ק	q ק	q ق	q
r 𐎗	r ר	r ר	r ر	r
š 𐎌	š/ś שׂ/שׁ	š/s/ś שׂ/ס/שׁ	š/s س/ش	š
t 𐎚	t ת	t ת	t ت	t
ṯ 𐎘	š שׁ	t ת	ṯ ث	š

TEXT DESIGNATIONS

Several different systems for numbering Ugaritic texts are currently in use. Of course, this unnecessarily complicates matters, but is nevertheless a reality. To facilitate your research, the different designations in the different systems for specific texts in the Baʿal and Anat cycle are provided below.

CTA: Herdner, Andrée. *Corpus des tablettes en cunéiforms alphabétiques découvertes à Ras Shamra-Ugarit de 1929 à 1939.* Paris: Paul Geuthner, 1963.

COS: Hallo, William W., ed. *The Context of Scripture.* 3 vols. Leiden: Brill, 2003.

CAT: Dietrich, Manfried, Oswald Loretz, and Joaquín Sanmartín. *The Cuneiform Alphabetic Texts from Ugarit, Ras Ibn Hani and Other Places*, Münster: Ugarit-Verlag, 1995. 2nd enlarged ed. of *KTU.*

KTU: Dietrich, Manfried, Oswald Loretz, and Joaquín Sanmartín. *Die keilalphabetischen Texte aus Ugarit: Einschliesslich der keilalphabetischen Texte aus ausserhalb Ugarits. Teil 1.* Alter Orient und Altes Testament 24/1. Kevelaer: Butzon & Bercker; Neukirchen-Vluyn: Neukirchener Verlag, 1976.

ANET: Pritchard, James B. *Ancient Near Eastern Texts Relating to the Old Testament, with Supplement.* 3rd ed. Princeton: Princeton University Press, 1969.

UT: Gordon, Cyrus H. *Ugaritic Textbook.* Analecta orientalia 38. Rome: Pontifical Biblical Institute, 1965. Rev. ed. 1998.

CTA	COS	CAT/KTU	ANET	UT	KTU (detail)
1	CTA 1	1.1	(VI AB)[7]		1.1
2	CTA 2	1.2	III AB B	137	1.2 i 1–47
			III AB C	129	1.2 iii 4–20
			III AB A		1.2 iv 5–32
3	CTA 3	1.3	V AB		1.3
4	CTA 4	1.4	II AB	51	1.4
5	CTA 5	1.5	I* AB	67	1.5
6	CTA 6	1.6	I AB	62	1.6 i 1–28; 1.6 vi 39–55
			I AB	49	1.6 i 29–vi 38

[7]Briefly described, but untranslated.

VOCABULARY LIST

This vocabulary list is not exhaustive. It provides you with all the words you will need to complete the exercises in this book. This list also supplies most of the words you will need to translate the texts of the Baʿal and Anat cycle. Occasionally, cognates (that is, corresponding words in other Semitic languages) for these Ugaritic words will be given in footnotes, especially where these are able to provide the rationale for the proposed vocalizations. Also, for verbs, the theme vowel for the *yqtl* is indicated in parentheses. Meanings for other than the G stem are provided following the standard abbreviation for the stem.

UNVOCALIZED	VOCALIZED	DEFINITION
ab	*ʾabu*	father
abn	*ʾabnu*	stone
adm	*ʾadamu*	humanity
adn	*ʾadānu*	father, lord
adr	*ʾadūru*[8]	mighty, majestic
adt	*ʾadāttu*	lady
ahbt	*ʾahabtu*	love
aḥd	*ʾaḥdu*	alone, only
aḥt	*ʾaḥḥattu*	one (f.)
aḫ	*ʾaḫu*	brother
aḫd	*ʾaḫida* (*a*)	to grasp, seize, take hold
aḫr	*ʾaḫra*	after, afterward
aḫt	*ʾaḫātu*	sister
ay	*ʾayyu*	which, any
ayl	*ʾayyalu*	deer
akl	*ʾakalu* (*u*)	to eat, consume; use
akl	*ʾaklu*	food
al	*ʾal*	not; used with jussive for negative command; surely
aliyn	*ʾalʾiyānu*[9]	(most) powerful
all	*ʾalilu*	garment
alp	*ʾalpu*	bull, ox
alp	*ʾalpu*	thousand
amr	*ʾamara*	Gt: to see (perhaps: to be seen)
amt	*ʾam(a)tu*	woman slave
amt	*ʾammatu*[10]	cubit
an	*ʾanā*	I

[8]Perhaps the passive participle. Cf. Akkadian *adāru* B "to fear, to respect, to be in awe" (*CAD* 1:108–109).

[9]This difficult form may be a superlative related to the verb *lʾy* "to be/become strong"; cf. Akkadian *leʾû* "to be able, to be powerful."

[10]Cf. Akkadian *ammatu* A "forearm, cubit" (*CAD* 2:70–75); and Hebrew אַמָּה (*ʾammâ*) "cubit."

any	*ʾanayyu*[11]	ship
ank	*ʾanāku*	I
anš	*ʾanaša*[12] (*u*)	to be weak
asr	*ʾasūru*	prisoner
ap	*ʾap*	also, moreover
ap	*ʾappu*	nose
aplb	*ʾappulibbi*	chest (*ʾappu* + *libbu*)
apn	*ʾāpanu*	wheel
apnk	*ʾappūnaka*	then, thereupon, next
apq	*ʾapīqu*[13]	stream
ar	*ʾāru*[14]	light
arbʿ	*ʾarbaʿu*	four
argmn	*ʾargamanu*[15]	tribute
arz	*ʾarzu*[16]	cedar
arḫ	*ʾarḫu*[17]	cow
arṣ	*ʾarṣu*	earth
arš	*ʾaraša*[18] (*u*)	to desire, request
at	*ʾatta*	you (ms)
at	*ʾatti*	you (fs)
atw	*ʾatawa*[19] (*u*)	to come, go
atm	*ʾattum*	you (mp)
aṯr	*ʾaṯara* (*u*)	to march
aṯr	*ʾaṯru*	place
aṯr	*ʾaṯra*[20]	behind, after
aṯrt	*ʾāṯiratu*	Athiratu
aṯt	*ʾaṯṯatu*	woman
ib	*ʾêbu*	enemy
ibr	*ʾibbīru*[21]	bull
idk	*ʾiddāka*	then, thereupon, next
iy	*ʾêya*	where?
ik	*ʾêka*	why?; how?

---

[11]Cf. Hebrew אֳנִיָּה (*ʾŏniyyâ*) "ship."

[12]Cf. Akkadian *enēšu*, and Hebrew אנשׁ (*ʾnš*) "to be weak, sick."

[13]Cf. Hebrew אָפִיק (*ʾāpîq*) "channel."

[14]Cf. Hebrew אוֹר (*ʾôr*) "light."

[15]Cf. Hebrew אַרְגָּמָן (*ʾargāmān*) "purple, articles of wealth, tribute"; and Akkadian *argamannu* "red/purple wool."

[16]Cf. Arabic أَرْز (*ʾaraz-*) "cedar."

[17]Cf. Akkadian *ʾarḫu* "cow."

[18]Cf. Akkadian *erēšu* "to desire."

[19]Cf. Arabic أتى (*ʾatā*) "to come, arrive."

[20]Cf. Arabic إِثْرَ (*ʾiṯra*) "immediately after, right after."

[21]Cf. Hebrew אַבִּיר (*ʾabbîr*) "strong, powerful, bull."

il	*ʾilu*	god, El
ilqṣ	*ʾilqaṣu*[22]	precious stone
ilt	*ʾil(a)tu*	goddess
imr	*ʾimmaru*	lamb
in	*ʾêna*	there is not
iqn	*ʾiqnu*[23]	lapis lazuli
irt	*ʾirtu*[24]	breast, core
išt	*ʾiššatu*	fire
iṯ	*ʾiṯê*[25]	there is
u	*ʾô*	or
ugrt	*ʾugarītu*	Ugarit
udm	*ʾudumu*	Edom
udn	*ʾudnu*	ear
udr	*ʾudru*[26]	caravan(?), quarry(?)
ul	*ʾôlu*[27]	mighty one
ulp	*ʾullūpu*[28]	chief
ulṯ	*ʾulaṯu*	trowel(?)
um	*ʾummu*	mother
umt	*ʾummatu*[29]	populace, tribe, clan
un	*ʾônu*[30]	mourning
uṣbʿ	*ʾuṣbaʿu*	finger
uṯpt	*ʾuṯpatu*	quiver
b	*bi-* (proclitic)	in, within, among; from, with, by (instrument)
bwʾ	*bāʾa*	to come, enter
bd	*bâdi/ê*[31]	in/from the hand/hands of
bht	*bahatu*	house
bky	*bakaya*[32] (*i*)	to cry, mourn
bkr	*bukāru*[33]	firstborn

---

[22] Perhaps related to Akkadian *algamišu* "steatite" (*CAD* 1:337)?

[23] Cf. Akkadian *uqnû* "lapis lazuli."

[24] Cf. Akkadian *ir(a)tu* "chest, breast."

[25] Cf. Aramaic אִיתַי (*ʾītay*) "there is, there are."

[26] The meaning of this word is uncertain. It may be related to the Akkadian *udru* "camel caravan," or Hebrew אַדִּיר (*ʾaddîr*) "majestic." Gordon, *Ugaritic Textbook*, 353, translates as "quarry."

[27] Tropper suggests this word is from **awl* (*Ugaritische Grammatik*, 252). Among others, de Moor translates it "the strength of the two of us" (*Religious Texts*, 39).

[28] Cf. Hebrew אַלּוּף (*ʾallûp*) "tribal chief."

[29] Cf. Akkadian *ummānu* "populace," and Hebrew אֻמָּה (*ʾummâ*) "tribe, clan."

[30] Cf. Hebrew אוֹנִי (*ʾônî*) "mourning."

[31] From *bi* + *yadi/ê* → **biyadi/ê* → *bâdi/ê*

[32] Cf. Arabic بَكَى (*bakā*) "to cry, mourn."

[33] Cf. Akkadian *bukru* "son, child"; and Hebrew בְּכוֹר (*bĕkôr*) "firstborn."

bl	*bal*	no, not, without
bmt	*bamatu*[34]	back, rear
bn	*bêna*	between, among
bn	*binu*	son
bny	*banaya* (*i*)	to build
bnš	*bunušu*	man, personnel
bʿd	*baʿda*[35]	behind, after
bʿl	*baʿlu*	lord, master, Baʿal
bqʿ	*baqiʿa* (*a*)	to split
br	*barru*	*meaning unclear*[36]
brḥ	*bariḥa*[37] (*a*)	to flee
brk	*birku*	knee
brq	*barqu*[38]	lightning
bšr	*bašara*[39]	to get tidings (D: to bring tidings)
bšrt	*bašartu*	good tidings
bt	*bêtu*[40]	house
bt	*bittu*	daughter
btlt	*batūlatu*[41]	virgin
bṯn	*baṯnu*[42]	serpent
g	*gû/î/â*	voice
gan	*gaʾānu*[43]	pride, eminence
gbʿ	*gabʿu*	hill
gly	*galaya* (*i*)	to leave
gn	*gannu*	garden
gʿr	*gaʿira* (*a*)	to rebuke, cry out
grš	*garaša* (*u*)	to drive out
d	*dū/dī/dā*	*the relative pronoun* (see p. 59)
dbb	*dabību*[44]	reptile
dbḥ	*dabḥu*	sacrifice, festival

---

[34]Cf. Hebrew בָּמָה (*bāmâ*) "back, hill."

[35]Cf. Arabic بَعْدَ (*baʿda*) "after."

[36]Cf. Akkadian *barru,* "gleaming, pure"; and Hebrew בַּר (*bar*) "pure." Thus, van Selms (*Ugarit-Forschungen* 7 [1975]: 472) assumes the existence of a Ugaritic noun *barru*, "the gleaming (metal)"; i.e., electrum.

[37]Cf. Arabic بَرِحَ (*bariḥa*) "to leave," and Hebrew ברח (*brḥ*) "to flee."

[38]Cf. Arabic بَرْق (*barq*-) "lightning."

[39]Cf. Hebrew בשׂר (*bśr*) "to bear tidings," and Arabic بَشَّرَ (*baššara*) "to announce, bring news."

[40]The plural of house (*bhtm*) should probably be vocalized as *bahatūma*.

[41]Cf. Arabic بَتُول (*batūl*-), and Hebrew בְּתוּלָה (*bĕtûlâ*) "virgin."

[42]Cf. Arabic بَثَن (*baṯan*-), Akkadian *bašmu*, and Hebrew פֶּתֶן (*peten*) "serpent."

[43]Cf. Hebrew גָּאוֹן (*gāʾôn*) "height, eminence, pride."

[44]Cf. Arabic دَبِيب (*dabīb*-) "reptile."

dgn	*dagānu*	Dagan
dwy	*dawiyu*[45]	sick, sickness
dyn	*dāna*[46] (*i*)	to judge
dkr	*dakaru*	male
dll	*dalīlu*[47]	fame, praise, glory
dlp	*dalapa*[48] (*u*)	to drop, drip
dlt	*daltu*	door
dm	*damu*	blood
dn	*dînu*	judgment
dᶜt	*daᶜtu*	message
dq	*daqqu*	small
dqn	*daqnu*[49]	beard
drdr	*dārdāru*[50]	eternity, generations
dry	*daraya*[51] (*i*)	to winnow, scatter, spread
drkt	*darkatu*[52]	dominion
drᶜ	*dariᶜa* (*a*)	to sow
ḏrᶜ	*ḏirāᶜu*	arm
ḏrt	*ḏartu*	dream, vision
hbr	*habara* (*u*)	to bow down
hdy	*hadaya* (*i*)	to lacerate, cut
hdm	*hadāmu*[53]	footstool
hw	*huwa*	he
hwt	*hawātu*[54]	word
hwt	*huwati*	him
hy	*hiya*	she
hkl	*hêkalu*	palace

---

[45]Cf. Arabic دَوًى (*dawan*) "sickness," and Hebrew דְּוַי (*dĕway*) "illness."

[46]Cf. Hebrew (*dîn*) דִּין "to judge."

[47]Cf. Akkadian *dalīlu* "fame, praise, glory."

[48]Cf. Hebrew דלף (*dlp*) "to drop, drip"; and Arabic دَلَفَ (*dalafa*) "to leak, drip, trickle." But cf. de Moor, *Religious Texts*, 40, n. 182, and Segert, *Grammar of Ugaritic*, 183, who argue for "to be shaky."

[49]Cf. Arabic ذَقْن (*ḏaqn-*) "beard, whiskers."

[50]Cf. Hebrew דּוֹר דּוֹר (*dôr dôr*) "generation after generation."

[51]Cf. Arabic ذَرَا (*ḏarā*) and Hebrew זָרָה (*zārâ*) "to winnow, scatter, spread."

[52]Cf. Arabic دَرَك (*darak-*) "attainment, achievement, accomplishment."

[53]Ludwig Koehler and Walter Baumgartner, *The Hebrew and Aramaic Lexicon of the Old Testament*. 5 vols. (Leiden: Brill, 1994–2000) 1:239, suggest *hadmu*; but Gordon, *Ugaritic Textbook*, 389, notes that the word has no Semitic etymology and offers evidence indicating the word is East Mediterranean.

[54]Cf. Akkadian *awātu* "word, command, affair, thing."

hl	*halā*[55]	here is; now
hlk	*halaka* (*i*)	to come, go, walk
hlm	*halama* (*u*)	to strike
hlm	*halumma*	here; behold; when, as soon as
hm	*himma*	if; or; whether
hmlt	*hamullatu*[56]	multitude
hmry	*hamārayu*[57]	flood, watery pit
hn	*hinnē*	Look! (attention grabber)
ht	*hitta*	now
w	*wa-* (proclitic)	and
zbl	*zabūlu*	prince
zr	*ẓâru*[58]	back part, top
zt	*zêtu*	olive
ḥbq	*ḥabaqa* (*u*)	to embrace
ḥdy	*ḥadaya* (*i*)	to see, look
ḥdr	*ḥuduru*[59]	room
ḥdṯ	*ḥadaṯu*	new
ḥwy	*ḥawaya*	Št: to bow down
ḥṭṭ	*ḥiṭṭatu*[60]	wheat
ḥẓt	*ḥaẓẓītu*[61]	lucky
ḥẓr	*ḥaẓīru*[62]	court(yard)
ḥy	*ḥayyu*	living, alive
ḥym	*ḥayyūma*	life
ḥkm	*ḥakama* (*u*)	to be wise
ḥkm	*ḥukmu*[63]	wise
ḥlm	*ḥulmu*[64]	dream
ḥmt	*ḥāmîtu*[65]	wall
ḥmr	*ḥimāru*	donkey
ḥmt	*ḥāmītu*	wall
ḥrb	*ḥarbu*	sword (f.)
ḥrr	*ḥarūru*[66]	baked/roasted thing

---

[55]Cf. Arabic أَلَا (*ʾalā*) "truly, indeed."

[56]Cf. Hebrew הֲמֻלָּה (*hămullâ*) "crowd."

[57]Cf. Hebrew מַהֲמֹרָה (*mahămōrâ*) "flood, watery pit."

[58]Cf. Arabic ظَهْر (*ẓahr-*) "back, rear."

[59]Cf. Hebrew חֶדֶר (*ḥeder*) "inner room."

[60]Cf. Akkadian *uṭṭatu* "wheat, barley"; and Hebrew חִטָּה (*ḥiṭṭâ*) "wheat."

[61]Cf. Arabic حَظِيَ (*ḥaẓīya*) "to enjoy the favor or good graces of someone."

[62]Cf. Hebrew חָצֵר (*ḥāṣēr*) "enclosure, court"; and Arabic حَظِيرَة (*ḥaẓīrat-*) "enclosure."

[63]Cf. Arabic حُكْم (*ḥukm-*) "wise."

[64]Cf. Arabic حُلْم (*ḥulm-*) "dream." However, Hebrew חֲלוֹם (*ḥălôm*) suggests *ḥalāmu*.

[65]Cf. Hebrew חוֹמָה (*ḥômâ*) "wall."

[66]Cf. Arabic حَرّ (*ḥarr-*) "heat, warmth."

ḥrš	*ḥarrāšu*	craftsman
ḥrṯ	*ḥaraṯa* (*u*)	to plow
ḫḫ	*ḫôḫu*[67]	decay
ḫym	*ḫayimu*[68]	tent
ḫlq	*ḫalaqa*[69] (*u*)	to perish
ḫmt	*ḫêmatu*[70]	tent
ḫmt	*ḫimʾatu*	butter
ḫss	*ḫāsasa*	L: to excite, arouse
ḫsr	*ḫasira*[71] (*a*)	to be lacking, absent
ḫrṣ	*ḫurāṣu*	gold
ḫtʾ	*ḫatiʾa*[72] (*a*)	to vanquish
ḫṯr	*ḫaṯru*[73]	sieve
ṭb	*ṭâbu*	good
ṭbḫ	*ṭabiḫa* (*a*)	to slaughter
ṭhr	*ṭuhūru*[74]	pure
ṭḥn	*ṭaḥina* (*a*)	to grind
ẓby	*ẓabyu*[75]	gazelle
ẓl	*ẓillu*	shadow
ẓr	*ẓêru*	top, back
y	*yā-* (proclitic)	vocative particle
ybl	*yabala* (*i*)	to produce, yield, bring
ybl	*yabūlu*	produce
ybmt	*yabimtu*	progenitor (f.)
yd	*yadu*	hand
yd	*yada*	with
ydd	*yadīdu*[76]	beloved
ydy	*yadaya* (*i*)	to scratch
ydʿ	*yadaʿa* (*i*)	to know

---

[67]Cf. Hebrew חוֹחַ (*ḥōăḥ*) in 1 Sam 13:6 "brier, bramble, thicket"; but parallels "caves, rocks, pits, and cisterns." But cf. Arabic خَوَّخَ (*ḫawwaḫa*) "to rot, decay, spoil."

[68]Cf. Arabic خَيْمَة (*ḫaymat-*) "tent." Because the *ay* does not contract to *ê* in Ugaritic, it must be followed by a vowel.

[69]Cf. Akkadian *ḫalāqu*, and Hebrew חלק (*ḥlq*) III "to disappear, vanish, perish."

[70]Cf. Arabic خَيْمَة (*ḫaymat-*) "tent."

[71]Cf. Arabic خَسِرَ (*ḫasira*) "to incur a loss."

[72]Cf. Akkadian *ḫatû* A "to smite" (*CAD* 6:151), and Hebrew חתה (*ḥth*) "to take away."

[73]Cf. Aramaic חֲשַׁר (*ḥăšar*) "to sift."

[74]Cf. Hebrew טָהוֹר (*ṭāhôr*) "clean, pure"; Arabic طُهُور (*ṭuhūr-*) "pomp, splendor, show, ostentation."

[75]Cf. Arabic ظَبْي (*ẓaby-*) "gazelle."

[76]Cf. Arabic وَدِيد (*wadīd-*) "favorably disposed, attached, devoted, fond."

ydʿ	*yadaʿa*[77] (*i*)	to sweat
ym	*yômu*	day
ym	*yammu*	sea
ymn	*yamīnu*	right, right hand
yn	*yênu*	wine
ysmt	*yasāmatu*[78]	beauty
ysr	*yasara* (*i*)	to chasten, instruct
yʿr	*yaʿru*[79]	razor
yṣʾ	*yaṣaʾa* (*i*)	to go out; D: to bring out
yṣq	*yaṣaqa* (*i*)	to pour out
yqy	*yaqaya*[80] (*i*)	to guard, protect
yrʾ	*yariʾa* (*a*)	to fear, be afraid
yrd	*yarada* (*i*)	to descend
yrḫ	*yarḫu*[81]	month; (new) moon
yrṯ	*yaraṯa*[82] (*i*)	to inherit, get
ytn	*yatana* (*i*)	to give, put, set
yṯb	*yaṯaba* (*i*)	to sit, dwell
k	*ka-* (proclitic)	like, as; at the time of
k	*kī-* (proclitic)	indeed, certainly
k	*kī*	because; when, if; that
kbd	*kabbada*	D: to honor
kbd	*kabidu*	heavy, serious, important
kbd	*kabidu*[83]	liver; interior, heart; middle, center
kbkb	*kabkabu*	star
kd	*kaddu*[84]	jar, pitcher
kḥṯ	*kaḥṯu*	chair, throne
kl	*kullu*	all, the whole
kll	*kālala*	L: to complete
kly	*kallaya*	D: to destroy
klt	*kallatu*[85]	bride
km	*kamā*[86]	like, as
kmn	*kumānu*	hectare

---

[77]Cf. Arabic وَذَعَ (*waḏaʿa*) "to flow."

[78]Cf. Arabic وَسامة (*wasāmat-)* "grace, charm, beauty."

[79]Cf. Hebrew תַּעַר (*taʿar*) "knife, small razor."

[80]Cf. Arabic وَقَى (*waqā*) "to guard, preserve."

[81]Cf. Akkadian *warḫu*, and Hebrew יֶרַח (*yeraḥ*) "month."

[82]But cf. Arabic وَرِثَ (*wariṯa*) "to inherit."

[83]Cf. Arabic كَبِد (*kabid-*) "liver; interior, heart; middle, center"; could also be vocalized as كُبود (*kubūd-*). Cf. also Hebrew כָּבֵד (*kābēd*) "liver."

[84]Cf. Akkadian *kandu* "a container of earthenware or silver, mainly for wine" (*CAD* 8:148).

[85]Cf. Hebrew כַּלָּה (*kallâ*) "daughter-in-law, bride."

[86]Cf. Hebrew כְּמוֹ (*kāmô*), and Arabic كَما (*kamā*) "as, just as."

kn	*kinna*	thus
kny	*kanaya*[87] (*i*)	to name
knn	*kânana*	L: to create (from *kwn*)
krkr	*karkara*	R: to twist, twiddle
krpn	*karpanu*[88]	goblet
krt	*keret/kirtu*	a righteous king in the epic literature
ks	*kāsu*[89]	cup, goblet
ksʾ	*kussīʾu*[90]	chair, throne
ksy	*kassaya*	D: to cover, put on
ksl	*kaslu*[91]	loins, back
ksp	*kaspu*	silver
kt	*kêtu*[92]	altar(?)
ktp	*katipu*[93]	shoulder
l	*lê-* (proclitic)	to, for, at; from
l	*la-* (proclitic)	used to introduce vocative
l	*lā-* (usu. proclitic)	not (general negative)
l	*lū-* (usu. proclitic)	verily, surely
lʾy	*laʾaya*[94] (*i*)	to cease, stop
lik	*laʾika*[95] (*a*)	to send (a message or messenger)
lim	*liʾāmu*[96]	(common) people
lb	*libbu*	heart
lbn	*labanu*	white
lbn	*labbana*[97]	D: to make bricks
lbn	*labinu*[98]	brick(s) (singular or collective)
lḥ	*lūḥu*	tablet (plural with -t)
lḥy	*laḥyu*[99]	cheek, jawbone (usually dual)
lḥm	*laḥima* (*a*)	to eat
lḥm	*laḥmu*	food, bread

---

[87]Cf. Arabic كَنى (*kanā*) "to name."

[88]Cf. Akkadian *karpa(n)tu* "pot, vase."

[89]Cf. Arabic كَأس (*kaʾsu*), Akkadian *kāsu*, and Hebrew כּוֹס (*kôs*) "cup, goblet."

[90]Cf. Akkadian *kussû* "seat, throne"; and Arabic كُرْسِي (*kursiy-*) "chair, throne."

[91]Cf. Hebrew כֶּסֶל (*kesel*) "loins" (collective).

[92]Meaning uncertain. Perhaps related to Arabic كَوى (*kawâ*) "to burn."

[93]Cf. Arabic كَتِف (*katif-*) "shoulder."

[94]Cf. Arabic لأي (*laʾaya*) "to be[come] weak."

[95]Cf. Arabic لأك (*laʾaka*) "to send as a messenger" and Hebrew מַלְאָךְ (*malʾāk*) "messenger."

[96]Cf. Hebrew לְאֹם (*lĕʾōm*) "people," and Arabic لَئيم (*laʾīm*), plural لِئام (*liʾām*) "ignoble, low, base."

[97]Cf. Arabic لَبَّنَ (*labbana*) "to make bricks."

[98]Cf. Arabic لَبِن (*labin-*) "brick(s)."

[99]Cf. Arabic لَحي (*laḥy-*) "jawbone."

lḥm	*laḥâmi*	cheeks
lṭpn	*laṭīpunnu*[100]	kind, benevolent, friendly
lṭš	*laṭaša*[101] (*u*)	to sharpen, burnish
ll	*lêlu*	night
llʾ	*laliʾu*[102]	kid
lm	*lêma*	why?
lpn	*lêpanî*	before, in front of, in/to the presence of
lpš	*lapūšu*[103]	garment
lṣb	*liṣbu*	narrow opening between rows of teeth(?)
lqḥ	*laqiḥa* (*a*)	to take, receive
lšn	*lišānu*	tongue
mid	*maʾda*[104]	very (much), greatly
mit	*miʾtu*	hundred
mbk	*mabbaku*[105]	spring, source
mgdl	*magdalu*	tower
mgn	*maggānu*[106]	gift
mh	*maha*	what?
mhr	*māhiru*[107]	skillful, expert
mzl	*mazala* (*u*)	to suffer
mḥmd	*maḥmūdu*	commendable, laudable, praiseworthy
mḫ	*muḫḫu*[108]	brains, marrow
mḫṣ	*maḫiṣa*[109] (*a*)	to strike, hit, kill
mṭr	*maṭara* (*u*)	to rain
mṭr	*maṭaru*[110]	rain
mẓll	*muẓlalu*[111]	shelter
my	*maya*	Woe!
my	*mīya*	who(m)?
my	*mayu*	water

---

[100]Cf. Arabic لَتيف (*laṭīf-*) "kindness, benevolence, friendliness."

[101]Cf. Arabic لَطَسَ (*laṭasa*) "to strike, hit"; and Hebrew לטש (*lṭš*) "to sharpen, smith."

[102]Cf. Akkadian *laliʾu* "kid."

[103]Cf. Hebrew לְבוּשׁ (*lĕbûš*) "garment, clothing, raiment"; and Arabic لَبوش (*labūs-*) "clothing, clothes."

[104]Cf. Akkadian *maʾda* "very (much), greatly."

[105]Related to Hebrew נֵבֶךְ (*nēbek*) "spring"?

[106]Cf. Arabic مَجّان (*majjān-*) "gratis."

[107]Cf. Arabic ماهِر (*māhir-*) "skillful, expert."

[108]Cf. Arabic مُخّ (*muḫḫ-*) "brain, marrow"; Akkadian *muḫḫu* "skull"; and Hebrew מוֹחַ (*môăḥ*) bone-marrow.

[109]Cf. Akkadian *maḫāṣu* "to strike, hit, wound, kill."

[110]Cf. Arabic مَطَر (*maṭar-*) "rain."

[111]Cf. Akkadian *muṣlālu* "midday rest," and Arabic مَظَلّة (*maẓallat-*) "sunshade, porch."

mk	*maka*	Behold!
mk	*môku*[112]	low
mknt	*makânatu*	place
mla	*mali*ʾ*a* (*a*)	to be full
mlak	*mal*ʾ*aku*	messenger
mlk	*malaka* (*u*)	to rule
mlk	*malku*	king
mlk	*mulku*[113]	kingship, reign
mlkt	*malkatu*	queen
mlit	*mali*ʾ*tu*	full
mn	*mannu*	which?
mnt	*munnatu*[114]	strength
mnt	*manatu*[115]	part, portion
msdt	*môsadatu*[116]	foundation
*m*ʿ	*ma*ʿ	enclitic after imperative
*m*ʿ*d*	*mô*ʿ*idu*[117]	appointed time, place (therefore, council)
mǵẓy	*muǵaẓẓiyu*	reward[118]
mǵy	*maǵaya* (*i*)	to reach, come, arrive
mpḫm	*mippāḫāmi*[119]	bellows
mṣbtm	*maṣbatāmi*	tongs
*mr*ʾ	*marī*ʾ*u*[120]	fat, fatling
mrkbt	*markabtu*	chariot
mrym	*maryamu*	height
mrr	*marara*[121]	to drive out
*mšb*ʿ*r*	*mušab*ʿ*iru*	torch (Š participle)
mwt	*māta* (*u*)	to die
mt	*môtu*	death, the god Môt
mt	*mutu*[122]	man, husband
mṯb	*môṯabu*[123]	dwelling

[112]Cf. Hebrew מוך (*mwk*) "to be low, depressed."

[113]Cf. Arabic مُلْك (*mulk*-) "rule, reign, kingship."

[114]Cf. Arabic مُنّة (*munnat*-) "strength, vigor, stamina."

[115]Cf. Hebrew מָנָה (*mānâ*) "part, portion."

[116]Cf. Hebrew מוֹסָד (*môsād*) "foundation."

[117]Cf. Arabic مَوعِد (*maw*ʿ*id*-) "promise; appointed time."

[118]See Johannes C. de Moor, *Ugarit-Forschungen* 1 (1969): 202 n. 6.

[119]Cf. Arabic مِنْفاخ (*minfāḫ*-) "bellows."

[120]Cf. Hebrew מְרִיא (*mĕrî*ʾ) "fatling."

[121]Cf. Arabic مَرّ (*marra*) "to pass."

[122]Cf. Akkadian *mutu* "man, husband, warrior"; and Hebrew מְתִים (*mĕtîm*) "males, men."

[123]Cf. Akkadian *mūšabu* "dwelling," and Hebrew מוֹשָׁב (*môšāb*) "seat, dwelling."

mṯn	*maṯnâmi*[124] (dual)	doubling, repetition
nbk	*nabaku*	spring
nbt	*nabbatu*[125]	adorned
nbt	*nūbtu*[126]	honey
ngš	*nagaša* (*u*)	to draw near, approach, meet
ngṯ	*naggaṯa*	D: to seek
nhr	*naharu*	river
nḥlt	*naḥlatu*	inheritance
nḥt	*naḥita*[127] (*a*)	to go down; D: to bring down
nwḫ	*nāḫa* (*u*)	to rest
nḫl	*naḫlu*[128]	wadi
nṭṭ	*naṭaṭa*[129] (*u*)	to leap(?); to wobble(?)
nǵṣ	*naǵaṣa*[130] (*u*)	to shake, tremble
nǵr	*naǵara* (*u*)	to guard[131]
nʿl	*naʿlu*[132]	sandal
nʿmy	*nuʿmayu*[133]	happiness, loveliness
npl	*napala* (*u*)	to fall
npr	*napru*	bird (collective)
nrt	*nûratu*[134]	luminary
npš	*napšu*	spirit, throat, life
nš	*nāšu*[135]	man
nšʾ	*našiʾa* (*a*)	to lift, raise
nšr	*našru*[136]	eagle
ntk	*nataka* (*u*)	to pour; Š: to cause to pour/rain
ntr	*natara*[137] (*u*)	to tear (a garment)
sʾn	*siʾnu*	hem(?)

[124]Cf. Arabic مَثْنِي (*maṯniy-*) "doubled."

[125]Cf. Arabic نَبَّتَ (*nabbata*) "to adorn."

[126]Cf. Hebrew נֹפֶת (*nōpet*), and Akkadian *nūbtu* "honey."

[127]Cf. Hebrew נָחֵת (*nāḥēt*) "to go down."

[128]Cf. Hebrew נַחַל (*naḥal*), and Akkadian *naḫlu* "wadi."

[129]Cf. Arabic نَطَّ (*naṭṭa*) "to jump, skip"; and Hebrew נוט (*nûṭ*) "to shake, tremble."

[130]Cf. Arabic نَغَصَ (*naǵaṣa*) "to disturb, ruffle, spoil."

[131]See John Huehnergard, *Ugaritic in Syllabic Transcription* (Atlanta: Scholars Press, 1987) 153.

[132]Cf. Arabic نَعْل (*naʿl-*) "sandal, shoe."

[133]Cf. Arabic نُعْمَى (*nuʿmā*) "happiness."

[134]Cf. Arabic نُور (*nūr-*) "light, lamp."

[135]Cf. Arabic ناس (*nās-*) "men, people, folks."

[136]Cf. Akkadian *našru* "eagle."

[137]Cf. Hebrew נָתַר (*nātar*) "to be free, loose"; Arabic نَتَرَ (*natara*) "to grab, grasp, wrest away"; and older Arabic "to rend a garment."

skn	*sakana*[138] (*u*)	to see to, take care of
spr	*sapara* (*u*)	to count
spr	*sipru*	document, tablet, text
srr	*sarara*[139]	to meditate
ʿbd	*ʿabdu*	slave, servant
ʿgl	*ʿiglu*[140]	calf
ʿglt	*ʿiglatu*	heifer
ʿd	*ʿadê*	up to, as far as, until
ʿdb	*ʿadaba*[141] (*u*)	to make, do, prepare, arrange
ʿdd	*ʿadīdu*[142]	homage, respect
ʿdn	*ʿadana* (*u*)	to appoint a time
ʿdn	*ʿiddānu*[143]	season, period of time
ʿdn	*ʿedinnu*[144]	plain
ʿḏbt	*ʿiḏḏabatu*[145]	merchandise
ʿwr	*ʿawwiru*[146]	blind
ʿz	*ʿizzu*	goat
ʿz	*ʿazzu*[147]	fierce, strong, mighty
ʿẓm	*ʿaẓmu*	bone
ʿẓm	*ʿaẓūmu*[148]	mighty, powerful
ʿyn	*ʿāna* (*i*)	to see
ʿl	*ʿalê*	on, upon, over; against; from on
ʿly	*ʿalaya* (*i*)	to go up
ʿlm	*ʿālamu*[149]	eternity, forever
ʿm	*ʿammu*	people
ʿm	*ʿimma*	with, in the company of; to, toward
ʿms	*ʿamasa* (*u*)	to load, carry; construct
ʿmq	*ʿimqu*	valley
ʿmr	*ʿamru*	dust(?), ashes(?)
ʿn	*ʿênu*	eye, spring, furrow

[138]Cf. Akkadian *sakānu* "to see to, take care of."

[139]Cf. Arabic سَرَّ (*sarra*) IV: "to tell under one's breath," "to whisper in someone's ear."

[140]Cf. Arabic عِجْل (*ʿijl-*) "calf."

[141]Cf. Hebrew עזב (*ʿzb*) II: "to put in order, arrange."

[142]Cf. Arabic عَزِيز (*ʿazīz-*) "mighty, powerful, respected."

[143]Cf. Arabic عَدّان (*ʿaddān-*) "period of time," and Hebrew עִדָּן (*ʿiddān*) "appointed time."

[144]Cf. Sumerian EDIN "plain, steppe"; and Hebrew עֵדֶן (*ʿēden*) II: "plain, Eden."

[145]Cf. Hebrew עִזָּבוֹן (*ʿizzābôn*) "merchandise."

[146]Cf. Hebrew עִוֵּר (*ʿiwwēr*) "blind."

[147]Cf. Hebrew עזז (*ʿzz*) "to be/appear strong."

[148]Cf. Hebrew עָצוּם (*ʿāṣûm*) "mighty," and Arabic عَظيم (*ʿaẓīm-*) "great, big, powerful, mighty."

[149]Cf. Arabic عَالَم (*ʿālam-*) "world, universe, cosmos"; and Hebrew עוֹלָם (*ʿôlām*) "long time, world."

ʿny	*ʿanaya* (*i*)	to answer, say; D: to humble; N: to be humbled
ʿnn	*ʿâninu*[150]	servant
ʿn	*ʿênu*[151]	spring (f.)
ʿnt	*ʿanata*[152]	now
ʿpr	*ʿapru*	dust
ʿṣ	*ʿiṣu*	tree
ʿṣr	*ʿiṣṣūru*[153]	bird
ʿqltn	*ʿaqallatānu*[154]	crooked
ʿr	*ʿêru*	ass
ʿr	*ʿîru*	city
ʿrb	*ʿaraba* (*u*)	to enter; to set (of sun)
ʿrpt	*ʿurpatu*	cloud
ʿrr	*ʿārara*	L: to arouse
ʿtq	*ʿataqa*[155] (*u*)	to pass
ǵḏḏ	*ǵaḏḏa*[156] (*u*)	to be strong, prevail
ǵzr	*ǵazru*[157]	hero
ǵly	*ǵalaya* (*i*)	to lower
ǵlmt	*ǵalmatu*[158]	young woman, maiden
ǵmʾ	*ǵamiʾa*[159] (*a*)	to be thirsty
ǵmr	*ǵamru*[160]	apprentice
ǵṣr	*ǵaṣīru*[161]	lush, luxuriant, fertile
ǵr	*ǵôru*	skin
ǵr	*ǵûru*[162]	mountain

---

[150]Cf. Arabic عَوْن (*ʿawn-*) "helper, aide, assistant; servant." But possibly related to Hebrew עָנָן (*ʿānān*) "cloud." For more detailed discussion, see van Zijl, *Baal: A Study of Texts*, 22, 102, and 104.

[151]Cf. Hebrew עַיִן (*ʿayin*) "spring."

[152]Cf. Hebrew עַתָּה (*ʿattâ*) "now."

[153]Cf. Akkadian *iṣṣūru* "bird."

[154]Cf. Arabic عَقَلَ (*ʿaqala*), and Hebrew עקל (*ʿql*) "to bend, twist."

[155]Cf. Arabic عَتَقَ (*ʿataqa*) "to pass."

[156]Gordon, *Ugaritic Textbook*, p. 463, maintains the meaning is unknown. Van Zijl, *Baal: A Study of Texts*, 152–53, 310, supposes that the root is cognate to the Hebrew עזז (*ʿzz*) "to be strong, prevail" due to the fact that the velar fricative *ǵ* in Ugaritic is represented by a pharyngeal fricative *ʿ* in Hebrew, and the Ugaritic *ḏ* by a *z* in Hebrew.

[157]Cf. Hebrew עזר (*ʿzr*) II: "young man, warrior, hero."

[158]Cf. Hebrew עַלְמָה (*ʿalmâ*) "young woman."

[159]Cf. Arabic ظَمِئَ (*ẓamiʾa*) "to be thirsty."

[160]Cf. Arabic غَمْر (*ǵamr-*) "inexperienced."

[161]Cf. Arabic غَضِير (*ǵaḍīr-*) "lush, luxuriant."

[162]Cf. Hebrew צוּר (*ṣûr*) "rock, cliff."

p	*pa*	and (sentence connector)
p	*pû/î/â*	mouth
pid	*piʾdu*[163]	mercy, kindness
pit	*piʾtu*	corner
pḏ	*paḏḏu*[164]	gold
phy	*pahaya*	to see
pḥl	*paḥlu*[165]	ass
pḫr	*puḫru*[166]	assembly, council
pl	*palla*[167]	to crack, notch, dent, plow
plṯt	*palṯatu*[168]	wallowing
pnm	*panûma*	face, presence (plural)
pnt	*pinnatu*	corner (of back=vertebra)
pʿn	*paʿnu*	foot
pʿr	*paʿira* (*a*)	to give/proclaim a name
pr	*pirû*	fruit
prsḥ	*parsiḥa* (*a*)	to collapse
prq	*paraqa* (*u*)	to break; to liberate
prš	*paraša* (*u*)	to spread out, overlay
prt	*parratu*	heifer
ṣat	*ṣiʾatu*	going forth
ṣbrt	*ṣubārati*[169]	team, band, group
ṣwd	*ṣāda*[170] (*u*)	to hunt
ṣḥq	*ṣaḥiqa*[171] (*a*)	to laugh
ṣḥrr	*ṣaḥrara*	to shine, scorch, roast
ṣyḥ	*ṣāḥa*[172] (*i*)	to shout, call
ṣwq	*ṣāqa*[173] (*i*)	Š: to press upon, seize
ṣlʿ	*ṣilaʿu*	ribs
ṣmd	*ṣimdu*	stick, war club
ṣmt	*ṣamata*[174] (*u*)	to destroy

---

[163]Cf. Arabic فُؤَاد (*fuʾād-*) "heart, mind, kindness."

[164]Cf. Hebrew פָּז (*paz*) "pure gold."

[165]Cf. Arabic فَحْل (*faḥl-*) "stallion."

[166]Cf. Akkadian *puḫru* "assembly, council."

[167]Cf. Arabic فَلّ (*falla*) "to dent, notch."

[168]Cf. Hebrew פלש (*plš*) *hitpaʿel*: "to roll about in mourning."

[169]Cf. Arabic ضُبَارَة (*ḍubārat-*) "collection, assembly."

[170]Cf. Arabic صَادَ (*i*) (*ṣāda*) "to catch, trap, hunt (down)"; and Hebrew צוד (*ṣûḏ*) "to hunt."

[171]Cf. Hebrew צחק (*ṣḥq*), and Arabic ضَحِكَ (*ḍaḥika*) "to laugh."

[172]Cf. Hebrew צוח (*ṣwḥ*) "to shout loudly."

[173]Cf. Hebrew צוק (*ṣwq*) *hipʿil*: "to constrain, press upon, harass."

[174]Cf. Hebrew צמת (*ṣmt*) "to destroy."

ṣʿ	*ṣāʿu*[175]	bowl
ṣrt	*ṣarratu*[176]	adversary
qblbl	*qibalbalu*[177]	sandal strap
qdm	*qudāma*[178]	before, in front of
qdqd	*qudqudu*	head
qdš	*qādišu*	temple functionary
qdš	*qudšu*[179]	holiness; sanctuary, shrine
qwm	*qāma* (*u*)	to rise
qṭn	*qaṭunu*[180]	small
ql	*qôlu*[181]	voice
qyl	*qāla*[182] (*u*)	to fall
qny	*qanû*	forearm, reed, shaft
qny	*qanaya* (*i*)	to acquire, create
qṣṣ	*qaṣṣu*[183]	cutting, hem
qrʾ	*qaraʾa* (*a*)	to call
qrb	*qaraba* (*u*)	to draw near
qrb	*qirbu*	midst
qrd	*qarrādu*[184]	hero
qrš	*qaršu*	abode, domain
qrt	*qarîtu*	city, town
qš	*qašû*[185]	chalice
qṯṯ	*qaṯṯa*[186]	to drag
riš	*raʾšu*	head, chief, top
rum	*raʾumu*[187]	buffalo, wild ox
rb	*rabbu*	great (substantive: great one)
rbb	*rababa* (*u*)	to be great
rbbt	*ribabātu*[188]	myriads

---

[175]Cf. Arabic صاع (*ṣāʿ-*) "bowl."

[176]Cf. Arabic ضرّ (*ḍarra*) "to harm." Cf. Tropper, *Ugaritische Grammatik*, 253.

[177]Cf. Arabic قِبالَ (*qibāla*) "opposite, face-to-face"—like straps?

[178]Cf. Arabic قُدّامَ (*quddāma*), Aramaic קֳדָם (*qŏdām*), and Akkadian *qudmu* "before, in front of."

[179]Cf. Arabic قُدْس (*quds-*) "holiness, sacredness; sanctuary, shrine."

[180]Cf. Akkadian *qatnu* "thin, younger."

[181]Cf. Arabic قَول (*qawl-*) "word," and Akkadian *qûlu* "speech."

[182]Perhaps related to Akkadian *qiʾālu* (of uncertain meaning). Cf. *CAD* 13:75–76.

[183]Cf. Arabic قَصّ (*qaṣṣ-*) "clippings, cuttings, chips, snips, shreds, scraps."

[184]Cf. Akkadian *qarrādu* "hero."

[185]Cf. Hebrew קַשְׂוָה (*qaśwâ*) "cup, chalice, jug."

[186]Cf. Arabic قَتّ (*qaṯṯa*) "to pull out, tear out, uproot."

[187]Cf. Hebrew רְאֵם (*rĕʾēm*) "wild ox."

[188]Cf. Arabic رُبّ (*rubba*) "many," and Hebrew רְבָבָה (*rĕbābâ*) "multitude, myriad, ten thousand."

rbt	*ribbatu*[189]	a myriad
rgm	*ragama*[190] (*u*)	to say
rgm	*rigmu*	word
rḥm	*raḥâmi*[191] (dual)	millstones
rḥm	*raḥima*[192] (*a*)	to be merciful
rḥm	*raḥimu*[193]	girl
rḥṣ	*raḥiṣa* (*a*)	to wash
rḥq	*raḥiqa* (*a*)	to be distant, far off
rkb	*rakaba* (*a*)	to ride
rʿy	*rāʿiyu*	shepherd
rǵb	*raǵiba*[194] (*a*)	to desire, hunger, crave
rpʾ	*rapaʾu*	shades/ghosts of the dead, deceased hero(?)
rqṣ	*raqaṣa*[195] (*u*)	Gt: to swoop, dance
š	*šû/î/â*	sheep
šil	*šaʾila* (*a*)	to ask
šir	*šiʾru*	meat, flesh
šbʿ	*šabiʿa*[196] (*a*)	to be satisfied; D: to satisfy
šbʿ	*šabʿu*	seven
šbt	*šāʾib(a)tu*	(water-)drawer
šbt	*šêbatu*[197]	gray hair
šd	*šadû*	field
šyt	*šāta* (*i*)	to put, place
škn	*šakana* (*u*)	to dwell; Gt: to establish; D: to set, impose; Š: supply
škr	*šakara* (*u*)	to hire
šlḥ	*šaliḥa* (*a*)	to cast, beat out (a metal)[198]
šlyṭ	*šaliyaṭu*[199]	powerful, mighty
šlm	*šalima* (*a*)	to be sound, whole, well
šlm	*šalmu*	welfare
šm	*šumu*	name
šmḫ	*šamiḫa* (*a*)	to rejoice
šmm	*šamûma*	sky, heaven(s)

---

[189]Cf. Arabic رُبَّ (*rubba*) "many," and Hebrew רְבָבָה (*rĕbābâ*) "multitude, myriad, ten thousand."

[190]Cf. Akkadian *ragāmu* "to call out, prophesy, summon."

[191]Cf. Arabic رَحًى (*raḥan*) "millstone."

[192]Cf. Arabic رَحِم (*raḥim-*, f.), and Hebrew רֶחֶם (*reḥem*) "uterus, womb."

[193]Cf. Arabic رَحِم (*raḥim-*, f.), and Hebrew רֶחֶם (*reḥem*) "uterus, womb."

[194]Cf. Arabic رَغِبَ (*raǵiba*) "to desire, crave"; and Hebrew רעב (*rʿb*) "to be hungry."

[195]Cf. Arabic رَقَصَ (*raqaṣa*) "to dance."

[196]Cf. Arabic شَبِعَ (*šabiʿa*) "to satisfy."

[197]Cf. Hebrew שֵׂיבָה (*śêbâ*), and Arabic شَيْب (*šayb-*) "gray hair, old age."

[198]See Gordon, *Ugaritic Textbook*, 490.

[199]Cf. Arabic سَلُطَ (*saluṭa*) "to have power or mastery over."

šmn	*šamnu*[200]	oil, fat
šmʿ	*šamiʿa (a)*	to hear, listen to, heed
šnt	*šanatu*	year
šnt	*šinatu*	sleep
špt	*šaptu*	lip
šyr	*šîru*	song
šrh	*šariha*[201] *(u)*	to flash, let loose
šrp	*šarapa (u)*	to burn
šty	*šataya (i)*	to drink
tbʿ	*tabiʿa*[202] *(a)*	to depart
tdrq	*tadraqu*[203]	tread
thmt	*tahâmatu*[204]	sea
tḥm	*taḥummu*[205]	message
tḥt	*taḥta*[206]	under, below, beneath; instead of
twk	*tôku*	midst (toward: *tôka*)
tlm	*talmu*[207]	furrow
tmn	*tamūnu*[208]	countenance, figure
tʿdt	*taʿûdatu*[209]	emmisary (one who gives testimony)
ṯat	*ṯuʾatu*[210]	ewe
ṯwb	*ṯāba (u)*	to return
ṯbr	*ṯabara*[211] *(u)*	to break
ṯbrnq	*ṯabaruniqu*	opening of the throat(?)
ṯlṯ	*ṯalaṯa (u)*	to plow
ṯlṯ	*ṯalāṯu*	three
ṯlḥn	*ṯulḥanu*	table
ṯm	*ṯamma*	there

---

[200]Cf. Arabic سَمْن (*samn-*) "fat," and Akkadian *šamnu* "fat, oil."

[201]Cf. Hebrew שָׁרָה (*šārâ*) "to let loose."

[202]Cf. Arabic تَبِعَ (*tabiʿa*) "to follow."

[203]Cf. Arabic دَرَقَ (*daraqa*) "to walk hastily."

[204]Cf. Akkadian *tâmtu* "sea, ocean"; and Hebrew תְּהוֹם (*tĕhôm*) "primaeval ocean, flood."

[205]For a discussion of this word, see Johannes de Moor, *The Seasonal Pattern in the Ugaritic Myth of Baʿlu According to the Version of Ilimilku* (Kevelaer: Butzon & Bercker; Neukirchen-Vluyn: Neukirchener Verlag, 1971) 102.

[206]Cf. Arabic تَحْتَ (*taḥta*) "under, below, beneath."

[207]Cf. Arabic تَلَم (*talam-*) "furrow." But cf. also Arabic تَلّ (*tall-*) "hill, elevation." In the latter case, the word would be vocalized as *tallūma* in the plural or *tallâmi* in the dual.

[208]Cf. Hebrew תְּמוּנָה (*tĕmûnâ*) "form, manifestation."

[209]Cf. Hebrew תְּעוּדָה (*tĕʿûdâ*) "testimony, attestation."

[210]Cf. Akkadian *šuʾātu* "ewe."

[211]Cf. Arabic ثَبَرَ (*ṯabara*) "to destroy, ruin."

ṯny	*ṯanaya* (*i*)[212]	to repeat
ṯpd	*ṯapada*[213] (*u*)	to set
ṯpṭ	*ṯāpiṭu*	judge
ṯql	*ṯiqlu*	shekel
ṯwr	*ṯôru*	bull
ṯrm	*ṯarama*[214] (*u*)	to eat, cut up
ṯrt	*ṯarratu*[215]	abounding in water
ṯtʿ	*ṯatiʿa*[216] (*a*)	to fear, be afraid

[212]Cf. Arabic يَثْنِي (*yaṯniyu*) "to double."

[213]Cf. Hebrew שפת (*špt*) "to set on."

[214]Cf. Akkadian *šarāmu* "to trim, cut to size."

[215]Cf. Arabic ثَرّ (*ṯarr*-) "abounding in water."

[216]Cf. Hebrew שתע (*štʿ*) "to be afraid."

ADDITIONAL BIBLIOGRAPHY

Grammars, Grammatical and Syntactical Studies

Bordreuil, Pierre, and Dennis Pardee. *A Manual of Ugaritic*. Linguistic Studies in Ancient West Semitic 3. Winona Lake, Ind.: Eisenbrauns, 2009.

Cazelles, Henri. *Précis de grammaire ugaritique*. *Bibbia e oriente* 21 (1979): 253–65.

Cunchillos, Jesús-Luis, and José-Ángel Zamora. *Gramática Ugaritica Elemental.* Madrid: Ediciones Clásicas, 1995.

Gordon, Cyrus. H. *Ugaritic Textbook.* Rev. ed. Analecta Orientalia 38. Rome: Pontifical Biblical Institute, 1998.

Israel, Felice. "Études de grammaire Ougaritique. Le dernière phase de la langue." Pages 255–62 in *Le Pays d'Ougarit au tour de 1200 av. J.C. Historie et archéologie. Actes du Colloque International, Paris, 28 juin –1er juillet 1993*. Ras Shamra-Ougarit 11. Edited by Marguerite Yon, Maurice Sznycer, and Pierre Bordreuil. Paris: Éditions Recherche sur les Civilisations, 1995.

Rainey, Anson. F. "Observations on Ugaritic Grammar." *Ugarit-Forschungen* 3 (1971): 151–72.

Schniedewind, William M., and Joel H. Hunt. *A Primer on Ugaritic: Language, Culture, and Literature*. Cambridge: Cambridge University Press, 2007.

Segert, Stanislav. *A Basic Grammar of the Ugaritic Language with Selected Texts and Glossary*. 4th printing with revisions. Berkeley/Los Angeles/London: University of California Press, 1997.

Sivan, Daniel. *A Grammar of the Ugaritic Language*. Handbuch der Orientalistik. First Series 28. Leiden: Brill, 1997.

Tropper, Josef. "Auf dem Weg zu einer ugaritischen Grammatik." Pages 471–80 in *Mesopotamica—Ugaritica—Biblica: Festschrift für Kurt Bergerhof.* Edited by Manfried Dietrich and Oswald Loretz. Neukirchen-Vluyn: Neukirchener; Kevelaer: Butzon & Bercker, 1993.

———. "Morphologische Besonderheiten des Spätugaritischen," *Ugarit-Forschungen* 25 (1993): 389–94.

———. "Themen der ugaritischen Grammatik in der Diskussion." *Ugarit-Forschungen* 33 (2001): 621–39.

———. "Ugaritic Grammar." Pages 91–121 in *Handbook of Ugaritic Studies*. Handbuch der Orientalistik. First Series 39. Edited by Wilfred G. E. Watson and Nicolas Wyatt. Leiden/Boston/Köln: Brill, 1999.

———. *Ugaritisch: Kurzgefasste Grammatik mit Übungstexten und Glossar*. Elementa Linguarum Orientis 1. Münster: Ugarit-Verlag, 2002.

———. *Ugaritische Grammatik*. Alter Orient und Altes Testament 273. Münster: Ugarit-Verlag, 2000.

Verreet, Eddy. *Modi Ugaritici: Eine morpho-syntaktische Abhandlung über das Modalsystem im Ugaritischen.* Orientalia Lovaniensia Analecta 26. Leuven: Peeters, 1988.

Translations (some with transliteration)

Caquot, André, Maurice Sznycer, and Andrée Herdner. *Textes ougaritiques: Tome I. Mythes et légends*. Littératures anciennes du Proche-Orient 7; Paris: Cerf, 1974.

Caquot, André, Jean-Michel de Tarragon, and Jesús-Luis Cunchillos. *Textes ougaritiques: Tome II. Textes religieux. rituels. correspondance*. Littératures anciennes du Proche-Orient 14; Paris: Cerf, 1989.

Cassuto, Umberto. *The Goddess Anath: Canaanite Epics of the Patriarchal Age*. Translated by Israel Abrahams. Jerusalem: Magnes, 1971.

Cohen, Chaim. "The Ugaritic Hippiatric Texts: Revised Composite Text, Translation and Commentary," *Ugarit-Forschungen* 28 (1996): 105–53.

Coogan, Michael D. *Stories from Ancient Canaan*. Philadelphia: Westminster, 1978.

Driver, Godfrey R. *Canaanite Myths and Legends*. Edinburgh: T. & T. Clark, 1956.

Fisher, Loren R., ed. *The Claremont Ras Shamra Tablets*. Analecta orientalia 48. Rome: Pontifical Biblical Institute, 1971.

Gibson, John C. L. *Canaanite Myths and Legends*. 2nd ed. Edinburgh: T. & T. Clark, 1978.

Gordon, Cyrus H.. "Poetics Legends and Myths from Ugarit." *Berytus* 25 (1977): 5–135.

Gray, John. *The Krt Text in the Literature of Ras Shamra*. Documenta et Monumenta Orientis Antiqui 5. Leiden: Brill, 1955.

———. *The Legacy of Canaan: The Ras Shamra Texts and Their Relevance to the Old Testament*. 2nd ed. Vetus Testamentum Supplements 5. Leiden: Brill, 1965.

Hallo, William W., ed. *The Context of Scripture*. 3 vols. Leiden: Brill, 2003.

Margalit, Baruch. *The Ugaritic Poem of Aqht: Text, Translation, Commentary*. Berlin: de Gruyter, 1989.

Moor, Johannes C. de. *An Anthology of Religious Texts from Ugarit*. Nisaba 16. Leiden: Brill, 1987.

Moor, Johannes C. de, and Klaas Spronk, *A Cuneiform Anthology of Religious Texts from Ugarit*. Semitic Studies Series. New Series 6. Leiden: Brill, 1987.

Olmo Lete, Gregorio del. *Mitos, leyendas y rituals de los semitas occidentals*. Barcelona: Edicions de la Universitat de Barcelona; Madrid: Editorial Trotta, 1998.

———. *Mitos y leyendas segun la tradicion de Ugarit*. Madrid: Ediciones Cristiandad, 1981.

Pardee, Dennis. *Ritual and Cult at Ugarit*. Writings from the Ancient World 10. Atlanta: Society of Biblical Literature, 2002.

———. *Les textes hippiatriques. Revista degli studi orientali* 2. Paris: Éditions Recherche sur les Civilisations, 1985.

———. *Les textes para-mythologiques de la 24e Campagne (1961). Revista degli studi orientali* 4. Paris: Éditions Recherche sur les Civilisations, 1988.

———. *Les textes rituels*. 2 vols. Ras Shamra-Ougarit 12. Paris: Éditions Recherche sur les Civilisations, 2000.

Parker, Simon B., ed. *Ugaritic Narrative Poetry*. SBL Writings from the Ancient World 9. Translated by Mark S. Smith, et al. Atlanta: Scholars, 1997.

Pritchard, James B. *Ancient Near Eastern Texts Relating to the Old Testament, with Supplement*. Princeton: Princeton University Press, 1969.

Smith, Mark A., ed. *The Ugaritic Baal Cycle*. Vol. 1. Vetus Testamentum Supplements 55. Leiden: Brill, 1994.
Smith, Mark A., and Wayne Pitard, eds. *The Ugaritic Baal Cycle*. Vol. 2. Vetus Testamentum Supplements 114. Leiden: Brill, 2009.
Wyatt, Nicolas. *Religious Texts from Ugarit: The Words of Ilimilku and his Colleagues*. 2nd ed. The Biblical Seminar 53. Sheffield: Sheffield Academic, 2002.

Lexicography

Greenfield, Jonas C. "Ugaritic Lexical Notes." *Journal of Cuneiform Studies* 21 (1967): 89–93.
Held, Moshe. "Studies in Ugaritic Lexicography and Poetic Style." Ph.D. dissertation, Johns Hopkins University, 1959.
Huehnergard, John. *Ugaritic Vocabulary in Syllabic Transcription*. Harvard Semitic Studies 32. Atlanta: Scholars, 1987.
Leslau, Wolf. "Observations on Semitic Cognates in Ugaritic." *Orientalia* 37 (1968): 347–66.
Koehler, Ludwig. "Problems in the Study of the Language of the Old Testament." *Journal of Semitic Studies* 1 (1956): 3–24.
Moor, Johannes C. de. "Ugaritic Lexicography." Pages 61–102 in *Studies on Semitic Lexicography*. Edited by Pelio Fronzaroli. Quaderni di Semitistica 2. Florence: Istituto di Linguistica e di Lingue Orientali, Università di Firenze, 1973.
Rabin, Chaim. "Lexicostatistics and the Internal Divisions of Semitic." Pages 85–102 in *Hamito-Semitica: Proceedings of a Colloquium Held by the Historical Section of the Linguistics Association (Great Britain) at the School of Oriental and African Studies, University of London, on the 18th, 19th and 20th of March 1970*. Edited by James Bynon and Theodora Bynon. The Hague/Paris: Mouton, 1975.
Renfroe, Fred. *Arabic-Ugaritic Lexical Studies*. Abhandlungen zur Literatur Alt-Syren-Palästinas und Mesopotamiens 5. Münster: Ugarit-Verlag, 1992.
———. "Methodological Considerations Regarding the Use of Arabic in Ugaritic Philology." *Ugarit-Forschungen* 18 (1986): 33–74.
Schall, Anton. "Eine Anscheinend übersehene ugaritisch-libysche Wortgleichung." Pages 399–403 in *Proceedings of the Fifth International Hamito-Semitic Congress 1987*. 2 vols. Edited by Hans G. Mukarovsky. Veröffentlichungen der Institute für Afrikanistik und Ägyptologie der Universität Wien 56. Beiträge zur Afrikanistik 40–41. Vienna: Afro-Pub, 1991.
von Soden, Wolfram. "Kleine Beiträge zum Ugaritischen und Hebräischen." Pages 291–300 in *Hebräische Wortforschung: Festschrift W. Baumgartner*. Vetus Testamentum Supplements 16. Leiden: Brill, 1967. Repr. pages 89–98 in *Bibel und Alter Orient: Altorientalische Beiträge zum Alten Testament von Wolfram von Soden*. Edited by Hans-Peter Müller. Beihefte zur Zeitschrift für die alttestamentliche Wissenschaft 162. Berlin/New York: de Gruyter, 1985.
Watson, Winfred G. E. "Ugaritic Lexicography." Pages 122–39 in *Handbook for Ugaritic Studies*. Edited by Winfred G. E. Watson and Nicolas Wyatt. Handbuch der Orientalistik. First Series 39. Leiden/Boston/Köln: Brill, 1999.

Dictionaries

Aistleitner, Joseph. *Wörterbuch der ugaritischen Sprache.* 4th ed. Berlin: Akademie Verlag, 1974.

Olmo Lete, Gregorio del, and Joaquín Sanmartín. *A Dictionary of the Ugaritic Language in the Alphabetic Tradition.* Revised ed. 2 vols. Leiden/Boston: Brill, 2003.

Concordances

Cunchillos, Jesús-Luis, et al., eds. *A Concordance of Ugaritic Words.* Translated by A. Lacadena and A. Castro. 5 vols. Piscataway, N.J.: Gorgias, 2003.

Dietrich, Manfried, and Oswald Loretz, *Word-List of the Cuneiform Alphabetic Texts from Ugarit, Ras Ibn Hani and Other Places: (KTU: second, enlarged edition).* Abhandlungen zur Literatur Alt-Syren-Palästinas und Mesopotamiens 12. Münster. Ugarit-Verlag, 1996.

Kottsieper, Ingo. "Indizes und Korrecturen zur 'Word-List of the Cuneiform Alphabetic Texts'." *Ugarit-Forschungen* 29 (1997): 245–83.

Whitaker, Richard. E. *A Concordance to the Ugaritic Literature.* Cambridge, Mass.: Harvard University Press, 1972.

Zemánek, Petr. *Ugaritischer Wortformenindex.* Lexicographie Orientalis 4. Hamburg: Helmut Buske Verlag, 1995.

Bibliographies

Cunchillos, Jesús-Luis. *La trouvaille épigraphique de l'Ougarit: 2. Bibliographie. Revista degli studi orientali* 5/2. Paris: Éditions Recherche sur les Civilisations, 1990.

Cunchillos, Jesús-Luis, Juan-Pablo Vita, and José-Ángel Zamora. "Ugaritic Data Bank: The Texts." Online: http://csic.academia.edu/JoseAngelZAMORA/Books/493255/The_texts_of _the_Ugaritic_data_bank_Ugaritic_Data_Bank. The_Text_with_english_commentaries_all_english_versions_.

Dietrich, Manfried, et al. *Ugarit-Bibliographie 1928–1966.* Alter Orient und Altes Testament 20/1–4. Kevelaer: Butzon & Bercker; Neukirchen-Vluyn: Neukirchener Verlag, 1973.

Dietrich, Manfried, and Oswald Loretz. *Analytic Ugaritic Bibliography 1967–1971.* Alter Orient und Altes Testament 20/5. Kevelaer: Butzon & Bercker; Neukirchen–Vluyn: Neukirchener Verlag, 1986.

———. *Analytic Ugaritic Bibliography 1972–1988.* Alter Orient und Altes Testament 20/6. Kevelaer: Butzon & Bercker; Neukirchen-Vluyn: Neukirchener Verlag, 1996.

Pardee, Dennis. "Ugaritic Bibliography." *Archiv für Orientforschung* 34 (1987): 366–471.

Smith, Mark. "A Bibliography of Ugaritic Grammar and Biblical Hebrew Grammar in the Twentieth Century." Online: http://oi.uchicago.edu/OI/DEPT/RA/bibs/BH-Ugaritic.html.

Loanwords and Relation to Other Semitic Languages

Avishur, Yitzhak. *Stylistic Studies of Word-Pairs in Biblical and Ancient Semitic Literatures.* Alter Orient und Altes Testament 210. Kevelaer: Verlag Butzon & Bercker; Neukirchen-Vluyn: Neukirchener Verlag, 1984.

———. *Studies in Hebrew and Ugaritic Psalms.* Jerusalem: Magnes, 1994.

Barr, James. *Comparative Philology and the Text of the Old Testament.* Rev. ed. Winona Lake, Ind.: Eisenbrauns, 1987.

Bennett, Patrick R. *Comparative Semitic Linguistics: A Manual.* Winona Lake, Ind.: Eisenbrauns, 1998.

Bergsträsser, Gotthelf. *Introduction to the Semitic Languages.* Translated and supplemented by Peter T. Daniels. Winona Lake, Ind.: Eisenbrauns, 1983.

Blau, Joshua. "Hebrew and North West Semitic: Reflections on the Classification of the Semitic Languages." *Hebrew Annual Review* 2 (1978): 21–44. Repr. pages 308–32 in *Topics in Hebrew and Semitic Linguistics.* Jerusalem: Magnes, 1998.

Brent, J. F. "The Problem of the Placement of Ugaritic among the Semitic Languages." *Westminster Theological Journal* 41 (1978): 84–107.

Cohen, Chaim. *Biblical Hapax Legomena in the Light of Akkadian and Ugaritic.* Society of Biblical Literature Dissertation Series 37. Missoula, Mont.: Scholars Press, 1978.

Dahood, Mitchell J. "The Linguistic Position of Ugaritic in the Light of Recent Discoveries." *Sacra Pagina* 1 (1959): 269–79.

Dhorme, Edouard. "La langue de Canaan." Pages 405–89 in *Recueil Édouard Dhorme: études bibliques et orientales.* Paris: Imprimerie nationale, 1951.

Fisher, Loren R, ed. *Ras Shamra Parallels. The Texts from Ugarit and the Hebrew Bible.* 3 vols. Rome: Pontifical Biblical Institute, 1972–1981.

Greenfield, Jonas C. "Amurrite, Ugaritic and Canaanite." Pages 92–101 in *Proceedings of the International Conference on Semitic Studies held in Jerusalem, 19–23 July 1965.* Jerusalem: The Israel Academy of Sciences and Humanities, 1969.

Greenstein, Edward L. "On a New Grammar of Ugaritic" (review of Daniel Sivan, *A Grammar of the Ugaritic Language*). Pages 397–420 in *Past Links: Studies in the Languages and Cultures of the Ancient Near East.* Israel Oriental Studies 18. Edited by Shlomo Isre'el, Itamar Singer, and Ran Zadok. Winona Lake, Ind.: Eisenbrauns, 1998.

Habel, Norman C. *Yahweh Versus Baal: A Conflict of Religious Cultures; A Study in the Relevance of Ugaritic Materials for the Early Faith of Israel.* New York: Published for the School for Graduate Studies, Concordia Seminary, St. Louis [by] Bookman Associates, 1964.

Haldar, Alfred. "The Position of Ugaritic among the Semitic Languages." *Bibliotheca Orientalis* 21 (1964): 267–77.

Hayes, John. "The Lexical Relationship between Epigraphic South Arabic and Ugaritic." Pages 609–26 in vol. 1 of *Semitic Studies in Honor of Wolf Leslau on the Occasion of his Eighty-fifth Birthday.* Edited by Alan S. Kaye, Wiesbaden: Harrassowitz, 1991.

Healey, John F. "L'ugaritique et l'étude des langues sémitiques." *Les Annales Archaeologiques Arabes Syriennes* 29–30 (1979–80): 17–22.

Healey, John F., and Peter C. Craigie. "Languages (Ugaritic)." Pages 226–29 in vol. 4 of *The Anchor Bible Dictionary*. Edited by David Noel Freedman. 6 vols. New York: Doubleday, 1992.

Hetzron, Robert. "La division des langues sémitiques." Pages 181–94 in *Actes du premier Congrès international de linguistique sémitique et chamito-sémitique, Paris 16–19 juillet 1969*. Edited by André Caquot and David Cohen. The Hague: Mouton, 1974.

———. "Semitic Languages." Revised by Alan S. Kaye. Pages 551–559 in *The World's Major Languages*. 2nd ed. Edited by Bernard Comrie. New York: Routledge, 2009.

———. "Two Principles of Genetic Reconstruction." *Lingua* 38 (1976): 89–108.

Huehnergard, John. "Languages (Introductory)." Pages 155–70 in vol. 4 of *The Anchor Bible Dictionary*. Edited by David Noel Freedman. 6 vols. New York: Doubleday, 1992.

———. "Remarks on the Classification of the Northwest Semitic Languages." Pages 282–93 in *The Balaam Text from Deir 'Alla Re-evaluated: Proceedings of the International Symposium held at Leiden 21–24 1989*. Edited by Jacob Hoftijzer and Gerrit van der Kooij. Leiden: Brill, 1991.

———. "Semitic Languages." Pages 2117–34 in vol. 4 of *Civilizations of the Ancient Near East*. 4 vols. Edited by Jack M. Sasson. New York: Charles Scribner's Sons/Macmillan Library Reference USA, 1995.

Isaksson, Bo. "The Position of Ugaritic among the Semitic Languages." *Orientalia Suecana* 38–39 (1989–1990): 54–70.

Kaye, Alan S. "Does Ugaritic Go with Arabic in Semitic Genealogical Sub-Classification?" *Folia Orientalia* 28 (1991): 115–28.

Korpel, Marjo Christina Annette. *A Rift in the Clouds: Ugaritic and Hebrew Descriptions of the Divine*. Munster: Ugarit-Verlag, 1990.

Leslau, Wolf. "Observations on Semitic Cognates in Ugaritic." *Orientaila* 37 (1968): 347–66.

Lewis, Theodore. *Cults of the Dead in Ancient Israel and Ugarit*. Harvard Semitic Monographs 39. Atlanta: Scholars Press, 1989.

Lipiński, Edward. *Semitic Languages: Outline of a Comparative Grammar*. Leuven: Peeters, 1997.

Marcus, Irvine David. "Aspects of the Ugaritic Verb in the Light of Comparative Semitic Grammar." Ph. D. dissertation, Columbia University, 1970.

Martinez, Ernest R. *Hebrew-Ugaritic index II with an Eblaite index to the writings of Mitchell J. Dahood : a bibliography with indices of scriptural passages, Hebrew, Ugaritic, and Eblaite words and grammatical observations, critical reviews, doctoral dissertations and related writings*. Subsidia Biblica 4. Rome: Biblical Institute Press, 1981.

Moor, Johannes C. de, ed. *Intertextuality in Ugarit and Israel*. Oudtestamentische studiën 40. Leiden: Brill, 1998.

Moscati, Sabatino, Anton Spitaler, Edward Ullendorff, and Wolfram von Soden. *An Introduction to the Comparative Grammar of the Semitic Languages: Phonology and Morphology*. Porta Linguarum Orientalium. New Series 6. Wiesbaden: Harrassowitz, 1964.

Olmo Lete, Gregorio del. “Fenicio y Ugarítico: correlación lingüística.” *Aula orientalis* 4 (1986): 31–49.

Page, Hugh R. *The Myth of Cosmic Rebellion: A Study of Its Reflexes in Ugaritic and Biblical Literature*. Leiden: Brill, 1996.

Pardee, Dennis. *Ugaritic and Hebrew Poetic Parallelism: A Trial Cut (ʿnt I and Proverbs 2)*. Leiden: Brill, 1988.

Petersen, Allan R. *The Royal God: Enthronement Festivals in Ancient Israel and Ugarit?* Sheffield: Sheffield Academic Press, 1998.

Rosén, Haiim B. “**Ekwos* et l’«hippologie» canaanéenne: réflexions étymologiques.” Pages 233–37 in *Studia Etymologica Indoeuropaea: Memoriae A. J. van Windekends (1915–1989) Dicata*. Edited by Lambert Isebaert. *Orientalia Lovaniensia Analecta* 45. Leuven: Departement Oriëntalistiek/Peeters, 1991.

Segert, Stanislav. “Le rôle de l’ougaritique dans le linguistique sémitique comparée.” *Ugaritica* VI (1969): 460–77.

Sivan, Daniel. “The Status of Ugaritic among the Northwest Semitic Languages in the Wake of New Research.” *Ugarit-Forschungen* 32 (2001): 531–41.

Tropper, Josef. “Is Ugaritic a Canaanite Language?” Pages 343–53 in *Ugarit and the Bible: Proceedings of the International Symposium on Ugarit and the Bible. Manchester, September 1992*. Edited by George J. Brooke, Adrian H. W. Curtis, and John F. Healey. Ugaritisch-biblische Literatur 11. Münster: Ugarit-Verlag, 1994.

Ullendorff, Edward. *Is Biblical Hebrew a Language?: Studies in Semitic Languages and Civilizations.* Wiesbaden : Harrassowitz, 1977.

van Zijl, Peter J. *Baal: A Study of Texts in Connexion with Baal in the Ugaritic Epics.* Alter Orient und Altes Testament 10. Kevelaer: Verlag Butzon & Bercker; Neukirchen-Vluyn: Neukirchener Verlag des Erziehungsvereins, 1972.

Voigt, Rainer M. “The Classification of Central Semitic.” *Journal of Semitic Studies* 32 (1987): 1–22.

Watson, Winfred G. E. “Non-Semitic Words in the Ugaritic Lexicon.” *Ugarit-Forschungen* 27 (1995): 533–58.

———. “Non-Semitic Words in the Ugaritic Lexicon (2).” *Ugarit-Forschungen* 28 (1996): 701–19.

———. “Non-Semitic Words in the Ugaritic Lexicon (3).” *Ugarit-Forschungen* 30 (1998): 751–60.

———. “Non-Semitic Words in the Ugaritic Lexicon (4).” *Ugarit-Forschungen* 31 (1999): 785–99.

———. “Non-Semitic Words in the Ugaritic Lexicon (5).” *Ugarit-Forschungen* 32 (2000): 567–75.

———. “Non-Semitic Words in the Ugaritic Lexicon (6).” *Ugarit-Forschungen* 38 (2006): 717–28.

———. “Non-Semitic Words in the Ugaritic Lexicon (7).” *Ugarit-Forschungen* 40 (2008): 547–70.

———. “Non-Semitic Words in the Ugaritic Lexicon (8).” *Ugarit-Forschungen* 42 (2010): 823–30.

Wright, William. *Lectures on the Comparative Grammar of the Semitic Languages.* Piscataway, N.J.: Gorgias, 2002.

EXERCISE ANSWER KEY

Lesson 2: Language Basics

1. *baʿlu*	Baʿal, lord
2. *ʿurpatu or ʿurpātu*	cloud *or* clouds
3. *yadu or yada*	hand *or* with
4. *ʾarṣu*	earth, land
5. *binu or bêna*	son *or* between
6. *pinnatu* or *pinnātu*	vertebra *or* vertebrae
7. *ʾêna*	there is not
8. *yammu* or *yômu*	sea *or* day
9. *ʾilu*	El, god
10. *bêtu* or *bittu*	house *or* daughter

Lesson 3: Nouns

1. *baʿlu ʾarṣi*
2. *pinnātu*
3. *bêta*
4. *binu ʾilīma*
5. *yômāmi*
6. *bêtu . . . baʿli*
7. *ʿênā baʿli*
8. *yadêmi*
9. *ʿurpāti*
10. *ʿênū ʾilīma . . . bêti baʿli*

Lesson 4: Adjectives

1. *ḫatūʾu* 1) verbal (passive), 2) masculine singular, 3) predicatively
2. *ḥayyu* 1) regular, 2) masculine singular, 3) predicatively

3. ***bāniyu*** 1) verbal (active), 2) masculine singular, 3) substantively
banūwāti 1) verbal (passive), 2) feminine plural, 3) substantively
4. ***šāmiḫu*** 1) verbal (active), 2) masculine singular, 3) predicatively
5. ***maḥrūṯāti*** 1) verbal (passive), 2) feminine plural, 3) attributively
6. ***kanūyāti*** 1) verbal (passive), 2) feminine plural, 3) attributively
7. ***qāniyati*** 1) verbal (active), 2) feminine singular, 3) substantively
8. ***laṭūšati*** 1) verbal (passive), 2) feminine singular, 3) attributively
9. ***ʾanāšātu*** 1) verbal (passive), 2) feminine plural, 3) predicatively
10. ***ḥukmu*** 1) regular, 2) masculine singular, 3) predicatively

Lesson 5: Prepositions

1. *Do not draw near* to the son of the gods
2. *Strike* between the hands of *Judge River*
3. The club *swoops* in the hands of Baʿal like an eagle
4. *My life was absent* among men
5. *She sets her face* toward the torch of the gods
6. *There is no* house for Baʿal like the gods
7. *You must set your* face toward *his city*
8. *They fall* under the feet of Baʿal

Lesson 6: Pronouns

1. ***ʾanāku . . . kaʾimmari bipîya***
   I *made him* like a lamb in my mouth

2. ***taḥummuka ʾilu ḥukmu***
   Your message, O El, is wise

3. ***maha . . . batūlatu ʿanatu***
   What *do you want*, O Virgin Anat?

4. ***. . . ʾilāma dā. . . .***
   Give, O gods, the one whom *you harbor*

5. *mannuma dabībīma dī môsadāti ʾarṣi*
   All manner of reptiles (which are) of the foundations of the earth

6. *ʾalʾiyā[nu] baʿlu ṯāpiṭunā*
   Powerful Baʿal, our Judge

7. *kalibbi ʾarḫi lêʿigliha*
   Like the heart of a cow is for her calf

8. *ʿênā baʿli qudāma yadêhu*
   The eyes of Baʿal are before his hands

Lesson 7: Verbs

1. *yipʿaru*	*yaqtulu*, 3ms	He names
2. *ʾanā banêtu*	*qatala*, 1cs	I built
3. *ʾatta timḫaṣu*	*yaqtulu*, 2ms	You will strike
4. *qaraʾtum*	*qatala*, 2ms	You called
qaraʾtumā	*qatala*, 2cd	You (two) called
5. *ʾamluku*	*yaqtulu*, 1cs	I shall rule
6. *huwa yimlaʾu*	*yaqtulu*, 3ms	He will fill
huwa yimlaʾ	*yaqtul*, 3ms	He filled
7. *ʾattum tilḥamūna*	*yaqtulu*, 2mp	You will eat
ʾattumā tilḥamāni	*yaqtulu*, 2cd	You (two) will eat
8. *maǵênayā*	*qatala*, 1cd	We (two) arrived
9. *ʾatti taṣmutīna*	*yaqtulu*, 2fs	You will destroy
10. *humā yiḫtaʾāni*	*yaqtulu*, 3cd	They (two) will vanquish

Lesson 8: Moods

Other vocalizations and translations are often possible.

1. *šmʿ lbtlt ʿnt* *š(a)maʿī labatūlatu ʿanatu*

Parsing:

MOOD	PERSON	GENDER	NUMBER
Imperative	2nd	feminine	singular

Translation: Hear, O Virgin Anat!

2. *mh taršn* *maha ta'rušīna*

Parsing:

MOOD	PERSON	GENDER	NUMBER
Indicative	2nd	feminine	singular

Translation: What do you want?

3. *tlḥm rpum* *tilḥamū rapa'ūma*

Parsing:

MOOD	PERSON	GENDER	NUMBER
Jussive	3rd	masculine	plural

Translation: Let the shades of the dead eat!

4. *ltikl* *lāta'kulū*

Parsing:

MOOD	PERSON	GENDER	NUMBER
Jussive	3rd	masculine	plural

Translation: Let them not eat!

5. *ym ymm yʿtqn* *yômu yômāmi yaʿtuqāni*

Parsing:

MOOD	PERSON	GENDER	NUMBER
Indicative	3rd	common	dual

Translation: A day, two days pass by.

6. *lḥm bṯlḥnt* *l(a)ḥam biṯulḥanāti*

Parsing:

MOOD	PERSON	GENDER	NUMBER
Imperative	2nd	masculine	singular

Translation: Eat from the tables!

7. *lpʿn mt hbr* *lêpaʿnê môti hbur*

Parsing:

MOOD	PERSON	GENDER	NUMBER
Imperative	2nd	masculine	singular

Translation: At the feet of Môt bow down!

8. *šmm šmn tmṭrn* *šamûma šamna tamṭurūna*

Parsing:

MOOD	PERSON	GENDER	NUMBER
Indicative	3rd	masculine	plural

Translation: The heavens rain oil.

9. *al tqrb* *ʾal taqrub*

Parsing:

MOOD	PERSON	GENDER	NUMBER
Jussive	2nd	masculine	singular

Translation: Do not draw near!

10. *bḥrb tbqʿnn* *biḥarbi tibqaʿannanū*

Parsing:

MOOD	PERSON	GENDER	NUMBER
Energic	2nd	feminine	singular

Translation: With a sword she (really) splits him.

Lesson 9: Infinitives

1. *maḫāṣuya himma maḫāṣu binîya* *Have you come* to slay me or to slay my sons?

2. *biyaṣāʾi nāšīma* In the going out of the men (= when the men go out)

3. *lêlaḥāmi walêšatāyi ṣaḥtukum* To eat and to drink I have called you (mp)

4. *mazālu yamzulu* Does he indeed suffer?

5. *tabāʿu ʾanāku* I departed

6. *yadāʿu lā yadiʿtu* I could not possibly have known

7. *wayaqrubu bišaʾāli kirti* And he drew near when Kirta asked (= in the asking of Kirta)

8. *šamāʿu ʾilatu* The goddess hears

Lesson 10: Thematic Stems

1. *ʿanatu tanaggiṯuhu*

ROOT	STEM	ASPECT or MOOD	PERSON/GENDER/NUMBER
ngṯ	D	*yqtl*	3fs (+ 3ms suffix)

Anat seeks him.

2. *ʾahabtu ṯôri taʿāriruki*

ROOT	STEM	ASPECT or MOOD	PERSON/GENDER/NUMBER
ʿrr	L	*yqtl*	3fs (+ 2fs suffix)

Does the love of Bull arouse you?

3. *šaskin maggāna*

ROOT	STEM	ASPECT or MOOD	PERSON/GENDER/NUMBER
skn	Š	imperative	ms

Supply the gift!

4. *ʾal tištaḥwiyā lêpuḫri môʿidi*

ROOT	STEM	ASPECT or MOOD	PERSON/GENDER/NUMBER
ḥwy	Št	jussive	2cd

Do not bow down to the assembly of the council!

5. *ʾarṣa darkati yištakinu*

ROOT	STEM	ASPECT or MOOD	PERSON/GENDER/NUMBER
škn	Gt	*yqtl*	3ms

He will establish a land of dominion.

6. *kaʾimmari bipîhu tiḫḫatiʾāni*

ROOT	STEM	ASPECT or MOOD	PERSON/GENDER/NUMBER
ḫtʾ	N	*yqtl*	2cd

Like a lamb in his mouth you will be vanquished.

7. *dūyašabbiʿu hamullāti ʾarṣi*

ROOT	STEM	ASPECT or MOOD	PERSON/GENDER/NUMBER
šbʿ	D	*yqtl*	3ms

The one who will satisfy the peoples of the earth

8. *kaʾiššatêmi yiʾtamirā*

ROOT	STEM	ASPECT or MOOD	PERSON/GENDER/NUMBER
ʾmr	Gt	*yqtl*	3cd

Like two fires they appear.

9. *yašattik baʿlu ʿênāti maḥrūṯāti*

ROOT	STEM	ASPECT or MOOD	PERSON/GENDER/NUMBER
ntk	Š	jussive	3ms

Let Baʿal cause rain to pour upon the plowed furrows!

10. *yibbanî bêtu lêbaʿli*

ROOT	STEM	ASPECT or MOOD	PERSON/GENDER/NUMBER
bny	N	jussive	3ms

Let a house be built for Baʿal!

Lesson 11: Weak Verbs

1. *tiʾḫadu*	from *ʾḫd*	She grasps
2. *tašaṣîqannahu*	from *ṣyq*	She seizes him
3. *taliku*	from *hlk*	She walks/goes
4. *ʾidaʿu*	from *ydʿ*	I know
5. *ʾaṯûbanna*	from *ṯwb*	I will return
6. *yašattik*	from *ntk*	Let him cause (something) to pour
7. *pallū*	from *pll*	They cracked
8. *kanūyātu*	from *kny*	named
9. *nāḫatu*	from *nwḫ*	resting
10. *taʿînu*	from *ʿyn*	She beholds
or *taʿîn*	from *ʿyn*	Let her behold
or *taʿnî*	from *ʿny*	Let her answer
or *taʿnû* (with triphthong)	from *ʿny*	She answers

Lesson 12: Adverbs

1. *ʾidākka ʾal tatinā panêma ʿimma ǵûri*

Then (the two of) you must surely set your faces toward the mountain

2. *hitta taṣmutu ṣarrataka* (or *ṣarrātika*: your adversaries)

Now you will destroy your adversary

3. *ʾappūnaka ʾalpa yiṭbaḫu*

Then he will slaughter an ox (or a thousand)

4. *maʾda timtaḫiṣanna* (3fs YQTL energic)

Much she smites

or *timtaḫiṣna* (2/3fp) you (fp) / they smite

or *timtaḫiṣīna* (2fs) you smite

or *timtaḫiṣūna* (2/3mp) you (mp) / they smite

or *timtaḫiṣāni* (2/3cd) you (cd) / they smite

5. *gâm yaṣîḫu ʾilu*

Aloud/loudly does El cry

6. *maǵaya qarêtah*

He came to the city

or *maǵayū* (3mp) they came; or *maǵayā* (3fp/md) they (two) came

7. *halaka ṯamma*

He went there

or *halakū* (3mp) they went; or *halakā* (3fp/md) they (two) went

8. *ʾaḫra tamǵiyāni malʾakā yammi*

ʾaḫra tamǵiyūna malʾakū yammi

Afterward come the two messengers of Yamm; or
Afterward come the messengers of Yamm

Lesson 13: Miscellanea

1. *ʾap ʿanatu tittaliku*

Also Anat walks about — Gt YQTL 3fs from *hlk*

2. *šêbatu daqnika lūtasiruka*

The gray hair of your beard surely instructs you — G YQTL 3fs + 2ms suffix from *ysr*

3. *ʾêna bêtu lêbaʿli*

There is no house for Baʿal

4. *walā yaṯabā / yaṯaba / yaṯabū / yaṯabā / yaṯibu*

(And) the two of them did not remain	G QTL 3md from ***yṯb***; or
(And) he did not remain	G QTL 3ms from ***yṯb***; or
(And) they did not remain	G QTL 3mp from ***yṯb***; or
(And) they did not remain	G QTL 3fp from ***yṯb***; or
(And) he does not remain	G YQTL 3ms from ***yṯb***

5. *ʾêya zabūlu baʿlu ʾarṣi*

Where is the Prince, the lord of the earth?

6. *maya hamullātu*

Woe, O multitudes!

7. *ʿadê ʾilūma tittalikūna šadâ*

Until the gods walk the field   Gt YQTL 3mp from ***hlk***

8. *lêpaʿnê ʾili ʾal tappulā / tappulū / tappul*

At the feet of El (you two) do not fall!	G Jussive 2cd from ***npl***; or
At the feet of El (you mp) do not fall!	G Jussive 2mp from ***npl***; or
At the feet of El (you ms) do not fall!	G Jussive 2ms from ***npl***

We want to hear from you. Please send your comments about this book to us in care of zreview@zondervan.com. Thank you.

ZONDERVAN®

ZONDERVAN.com/
AUTHORTRACKER
follow your favorite authors

CPSIA information can be obtained at www.ICGtesting.com
Printed in the USA
LVOW09s0047260215

428359LV00006B/53/P

9 780310 495925